handcrafted soap

handcrafted soap

DELORES BOONE

NORTH LIGHT BOOKS
CINCINNATI, OHIO
www.artistsnetwork.com

About the Author

Delores Boone is a registered nurse who left the health care profession in 1991. In 1999 she and her husband, Don, started Boone's Lather Soap Company. In addition to selling custom-made soaps and toiletries, she teaches soapmaking classes and maintains a soapmaking Internet group. The Boones have six children and seven grandchildren. They reside in Monroe, Washington.

Handcrafted Soap. © 2002 by Delores Boone. Manufactured in China. All rights reserved. No part of this book may be reproduced in any form or by any electronic or mechanical means including information storage and retrieval systems without permission in writing from the publisher, except by a reviewer, who may quote brief passages in a review. Published by North Light Books, an imprint of F&W Publications, Inc., 4700 East Galbraith Road, Cincinnati, Ohio 45236. (800) 289-0963. First edition.

Other fine North Light books are available from your local bookstore or art supply store or direct from the publisher.

05 04 03 02   5 4 3 2 1

Library of Congress Cataloging-in-Publication Data
Boone, Delores.
    Handcrafted soap/ by Delores Boone
        p. cm.
    Includes index.
    ISBN 1-58180-268-4 (pbk. : alk. paper)
    1. Soap. I. Title

TP991 .B58 2002
668'.12--dc21

                                        2002070855

Editor: Catherine Cochran
Designer: Stephanie Strang
Production coordinator: Sara Dumford
Production artist: Cheryl VanDeMotter
Photographers: Tim Grondin, Christine Polomsky and Al Parrish
Photo Stylist: Jan Nickum

First and foremost, I dedicate this book to the Lord for giving me the opportunity to share my love of soapmaking. To my family, Don, Donelle and Warren, for the sacrifices they made and for investing time with me. To the best dad in the world, Ralph E. Kirkwood, who showed me I could do anything I set my mind to. To my Hot Soap Etc. "family," who faithfully kept this group running smoothly while I worked on this book. To you, the reader, because without your interest, this book would not have been possible. Last, but never least, to my soapmaking "sister" Nardi Lehnert, who I know loves and supports me with an unconditional love—no matter what.

✺ *Thank you*

to North Light Books and my editors, Maggie Moschell and Catherine Cochran, for your confidence and foresight in this book.

And thank you to the vendors who generously supplied materials for the photo shoot:

• Will and Doreen Knott from Old Will Knot for the scale.

• Andy Wenner from Wenner's Wood & Metal, Inc., for the large log mold and miter box cutter.

• Jan Schmidt from Sweet Prairie Soap Company for the smaller log mold.

• Rebecca and Chris Harder from the Sunnybrook Soap Company for the box mold and trowel.

• Mike Lawson from Columbus Foods Company for the generous supply of olive, avocado, almond, castor, coconut and palm kernel base oils.

• Catherine Failor from Milky Way Molds, Inc., for the plastic goat's head molds.

• Zenith Supplies for the shampoo bar essential oils and shea butter.

• Life of the Party for donating the Melt & Pour base soap.

• Anne Marie from Bramble Berry, Inc., for the chamomile bergamot fragrance oil and plastic cavity molds.

• Kaila Westerman from TKB Trading, LCC for sending colorants.

• Noel at A Garden Eastward, who so generously gave permission to use and add to the Essential Oil Blending Characteristics Chart.

CONTENTS ❁

introduction

Make soap? Why in the world would anyone want to make soap? That is what I thought at one time. I was spending the day with my friend, and she asked if I wanted to help her make soap. I agreed, but I silently groaned. During the hour it took to blend the oils, distilled water and lye into a pudding-like mixture, I was bored to tears. Why would I want to stand in front of this hot pot, stirring and pouring the mixture into molds, when I can easily go out and buy soap? My friend was so excited and enthusiastic, so I kept silent. When I left, she gave me a bar of the soap we made. The soap felt familiar—sort of. It was hard, but misshapen. And the soap was exotically fragrant, unlike the familiar nondescript fragrance I was used to with store-bought soaps. I thanked her as enthusiastically as possible for someone with no interest in soapmaking. I drove home thinking up excuses should she ever catch me off guard wanting to make soap again. Sure the soap smelled good, and there was the feeling of accomplishment at making it, but soap is soap, right? I have more productive ways to spend my time.

The first time I used this handcrafted soap, I was surprised by the way it lathered and amazed at how creamy it felt. More than that, I was awestruck at how squeaky-clean I was. Even my husband noticed how soft and smooth my skin felt. This was not at all like store-bought soap. The handcrafted soap felt more luxurious on my skin and stirred my senses. Once I tried it, I became a convert.

Although I loved the finished bar of soap, I wanted to find an easier and faster way to make soap. Experimenting with my electric slow cooker, I made a batch of soap in about an hour! This new method, called hot-process, uses an indirect heat source to cook the soap mixture. This is a tremendous improvement to the cold-process method which does not use a heating element and it takes weeks for the soap to cure and harden on its own. This new hot-process method opened a whole new way of soapmaking for me that was enjoyable! Eventually, I began to experiment with an array of soapmaking recipes. I experimented with different oils for my skin type, which is the "I am getting older and drier" type. I figured out different properties of different oils, which oils work best together and which oils are the most moisturizing.

All of this sounds like you have to be an expert in chemistry—but don't worry—even the most inexperienced crafter can pamper herself with a luxurious bar of handmade soap. I have provided you with several recipes that you can follow step-by-step. Once you get the hang of soapmaking—and I'm sure you will—I have also included the necessary charts and information for you to design your own recipes. Handmade soap makes a unique gift for friends and family, but you may just want to keep it for yourself!

Soapmaking is a chemical reaction involving lye, distilled water and oils or fats. The following pages will outline basic information about soapmaking, including the precise ingredients, equipment and supplies you will need to safely make soap.

What Is Soap?

True soap is a cleaning agent made up solely of fats or oils, distilled water and lye. There are many methods to making soap, but it always involves these three ingredients. When oil

is mixed with lye and distilled water, a chemical reaction takes place. This process is called saponification. The molecules separate and reattach themselves in a different pattern, making a totally new substance called soap. While you may use a variety of combinations of oils, fragrances and color additives to get a variety of types of soap, the basic formula will always remain the same.

True soap is nothing new. Our great-great-grandmothers made it on the farm, usually out of lard or tallow, water and lye made from wood ash. The amount of lye was difficult to regulate. The result was lye-heavy soaps, which often caused severe skin irritations.

Today all of the ingredients you need for soapmaking can be found at your local grocery, craft or hardware stores. After several generations, soapmaking has become a popular hobby pursued by many beginners and experienced enthusiasts not only because they take pride in making something with their hands, but also because true soap is so luxurious and healthy for your skin.

What Have You Been Washing With?

You may still have your doubts about soapmaking. You've heard it's messy or dangerous, with unpredictable results. Why not just go to the store and buy some soap? For those of you with doubts, I suggest you try true soap one time, and you will never want to use store-bought soap again. What you buy in the store is actually a synthetic detergent. It is mild enough for your skin and cleans your body well; however, there is no comparison between true soap and these synthetic detergents. After World War II, synthetic detergents were produced more and more. Manufacturers produced a variety of industrial cleaners, lubricants, domestic laundry and body cleansing agents because it was more economical. Cleansing bars work. They are pleasant enough and do the job. But, over time many of us have discovered that clean is not always enough. We want to pamper our skin.

Soapmaking Today

Soap has also come full circle. Granny's lye soap evolved into bar soap made by manufacturers. Then World War II began and manufacturers started to make synthetic detergents due to the needs of the time. They just never switched back after the war, because it was more economical.

Soapmaking has become a very popular craft in a large part because people want to treat and nourish their skin. You can find most of the necessary soapmaking supplies easily, and with the hot-process method, you will have a bar of soap in a few hours. What was once a very long and tedious process, soapmaking is now quick, easy, safe and foolproof.

Not only will your skin feel soft and smooth with the soap that you make from scratch, you will have a tremendous feeling of accomplishment, knowing that you made something that is good for you!

Important Terms to Know

Before learning how to make soap, it is important to understand the basic terms and techniques.

Trace

When you initially combine the oils with lye and distilled water, you blend it together until it thickens. Trace is the thickening of the oil, water and lye mixture. At this point, the molecules attach themselves together to turn into soap.

Saponification

This is the general term for the entire chemical reaction of oils, distilled water and lye turning into soap. When you put these ingredients together, the molecules separate and then rearrange themselves in an entirely new way, forming soap.

Curing

In older soapmaking methods, the soap must cure in molds to reach saponification. With the hot-process methods featured in this book, curing is finished once the soap has finished cooking. After saponification, the soap is ready to mold. Add the soap to the molds of your choice and let it harden. In a few hours, most soaps will be ready to use. Other recipes, like Spanish castile soap, produce a better bar of soap if it sits in the mold and hardens for up to three months.

Superfatting

Superfatting is the way to ensure that you do not produce a lye-heavy soap. Once the oils react with the lye and distilled water, there should be no leftover lye. Active lye in your soap can be very irritating to your skin. Basically, superfatting is providing a cushion of extra oil that will not be saponified. This protects against slight miscalculations that can occur due to scale fluctuations. A common amount to superfat is between 5%–7%. Superfatting also makes soap milder and more moisturizing to your skin.

Soapmaking Methods

True soap can be made a variety of ways. While the recipes and instructions in this book are all for hot-process soapmaking, it is important to understand the difference between hot process and cold process.

Cold Process

One of the most common methods of making soap is called cold process. With the cold-process method, you combine the oils, distilled water and lye and bring the mixture to trace. Next, you add fragrance oils and put it in the mold while it is still pourable. Saponification actually takes place in the mold. After a few weeks, the soap cures and hardens.

There are a few disadvantages to this method. First of all, it takes a prolonged amount of time for the soap to harden. It can be inconvenient finding a spot to store the soap while it saponifies and cures, and besides, who wants to wait a few weeks before you can use your soap? Another disadvantage with this method is that you need twice as much fragrance or essential oils, which can be costly. When the lye and oils combine, the chemical reaction produces heat. Once you add the fragrance to the mixture, it often dissipates because of this heat. The most noted problem occurs if active lye and the fragrances react with each other. The soap may suddenly thicken, curdle or the oils may separate and not mix back together. This is called seizing.

Hot Process

The newest trend in soapmaking is the hot-process method. It is a much easier and convenient way to make soap. To make soap the hot-process way, simply combine the oil, distilled water and lye. Stir the soap mixture to trace. Then you cook the soap using indirect heat (that is, the heating element does not come into direct contact with the soap). Indirect heat is a more predictable way to ensure a successful batch of soap. After the soap mixture has cooked, stir to cool slightly, then add the fragrance and put it in the molds.

There are many advantages to making hot-process soap. The soap mixture saponifies in about an hour, as opposed to a few weeks. You literally could make soap in the morning and use it in the shower that very evening. Also, another advantage is that you save money on fragrance oils and essential oils. Because you add the fragrance after the soap has cooled, you don't lose any from the active lye. Another advantage of hot-process over cold-process soapmaking is that you don't have to worry about seizing. The soap has already saponified by the time you add the fragrance.

All soapmaking ingredients have unique characteristics. Therefore, it is important to follow the recipes exactly as they are given in the book. Some oil combinations produce a harder bar of soap, while others produce a softer bar. Some oils are moisturizing, while others are not. It is important to familiarize yourself with all of these ingredients before you begin the soapmaking process.

Oils and fats may look alike, but can be vastly different in feel and performance. To make soap, you need oils and/or fats, distilled water and lye.

Oils and Fats

When you make soap, the first ingredients to look for are your oils. In soapmaking, you may use either plant-based oils or animal fats. The oils you use will determine what kind of soap you make. Some oils like grapeseed oil will produce a soft soap, while other oils, such as coconut oil, will produce a rock-hard bar of soap. The oils you use will also determine the structure of the soap. Emu oil and avocado oil will condition and nourish your skin, whereas olive oil and castor oil draw moisture from the air to help moisturize your skin. Conversely, palm kernel oil is not moisturizing at all. By combining several oils, you balance out the characteristics and create a bar of soap that is hard enough to last in the shower, soft enough to mold easily, and will cleanse and soften your skin.

Vegetable Oils

Most of the recipes included in this book call for plant-based oils. These are the more common oils used in the recipes in this book. For a more complete list, refer to the Charts & References section on pages 110–120.

• almond oil

This is a relatively inexpensive oil that adds excellent skin conditioners to a recipe. It is a clear liquid at room temperature and can help to produce a white bar of soap.

• avocado oil

This is a must-have oil because it is one of the best conditioning oils. It is a pale green oil that is high in unsaponifiables, which means that part of the oil will not turn into soap, no matter how much lye you add. Use this oil in recipes to replenish damaged skin and hair.

• canola oil

Canola is a great filler oil and very economical. While it is not one of the better conditioners, it helps to maintain a hard, white bar of soap.

• castor oil

This oil gives you a rich, creamy lather and concentrated conditioning. This is a humectant oil, which means it draws moisture from the air. Use 1–4 ounces (30ml–120ml) per recipe to provide excellent skin conditioning.

• cocoa butter

While cocoa butter can be very conditioning, too much of it can feel drying. It is a very hard solid at room temperature, but will give your soap a creamy feel. Unrefined cocoa butter has a chocolate scent.

• coconut oil

This oil is a soapmaking staple because it hardens a bar of soap better than any other oil, and makes a lather full of big bubbles. This oil is solid at room temperature and makes a white bar of soap.

• grapeseed oil

Grapeseed oil comes in various shades of green. It is a very thin liquid oil at room temperature. This oil softens soap slightly and is a lightweight skin conditioner. Often this oil is used in aromatherapy or massage.

• jojoba

Jojoba is actually a wax and not a true oil. It helps to maintain the skin's moisture and coat damaged hair shafts. Jojoba can be clear to golden yellow, depending on how much it has been refined.

• olive oil

This is another must-have oil. It comes in various shades of green, depending on the grades—extra virgin to pomace. It is a neutral oil, so it will not actively harden or soften a bar of soap. It helps to bring out the characteristics of the other oils in the recipes.

• palm kernel oil

This is another must-have oil because of its hardening power, behaving similarly to coconut oil, but slightly milder. This oil makes a great lather full of big bubbles. Using this oil will help produce a white bar of soap.

• safflower oil

Safflower oil provides light skin conditioning and rinses clean. It is a transparent, light-colored oil, liquid at room temperature. This oil is good for maintaining a white bar of soap. Generally, you only need 6–8 ounces (180ml–240ml) per recipe because too much will soften the soap. In humid and warmer climates, this oil will break down because of the heat, so you may want to buy a safflower oil high in oleic acid.

• shea butter

This is a white butter, solid at room temperature. It wonderfully softens your skin because it is high in unsaponifiables. Shea butter can be refined or unrefined.

*Where can I find the oils
I need to make soap?*

The easiest place to find most of the oils used in soapmaking is the grocery store. The next time you are shopping for groceries, go to the baking section, gourmet food section, ethnic food section and perhaps even the refrigerated or meat department. Look at the variety of oils available. Make sure you read the fine print. Often vegetable oil is mostly soy but may contain several other oils as well. Be sure to avoid combination oils when making soap, because it is virtually impossible to calculate the correct amount of lye. Most of the time you can find soy, corn, grapeseed, canola, sunflower, avocado, olive, safflower oils and lard at your local grocery store.

For more exotic oils, like coconut oil and cocoa butter, look in health food stores or wholesale grocers. You may also refer to the Resources section on pages 122–124 for oil suppliers.

• **sunflower oil**
This oil is similar to safflower oil but will soften the soap even more. It is great to add to recipes because it rinses clean.

• **wheat germ oil**
Wheat germ oil has a slight medicinal smell, even when refined. It is an orange liquid at room temperature and will discolor your soap. Only 2–4 ounces (60ml–120ml) are necessary in a recipe to feel its effect.

Animal Fats

Animal fats are often used in the soapmaking process. Most of the recipes listed in this book are made with vegetable oils, but animal fats are an economical alternative. For recipes using animal fats, see page 99.

• **emu oil**
There are two grades of emu oil: cosmetic (white) or soap (pale yellow). It is a opaque liquid at room temperature. While emu oil does not actively harden or soften soap, it provides extraordinary skin conditioning. It soothes and heals the skin, and it is the only animal oil that is noncomedogenic (won't clog your pores).

• **lard and tallow**
Lard is the fat of a pig and tallow is rendered from beef fat (suet). Ask your local butcher for suet or buy it from a company that sells it prerendered. Lard is available at the grocery store. Animal fats are good for hardening soap and producing a mild bar with decent suds.

Lye and Distilled Water

Lye is also known as caustic soda or sodium hydroxide. It is a caustic alkaline substance, similar to bleach. It is most commonly found in hardware or grocery stores, where you find the drain openers. Be sure you buy pure lye and not commercial drain openers, which may contain other chemicals. You need lye for each and every batch of soap you make. No lye, no soap. No lie.

Another essential ingredient is distilled water, which is found in grocery stores. Be sure that you do not substitute regular tap water for distilled water. Some tap water may contain minerals that could react with the lye and ruin your soap.

In soapmaking, one of the first steps requires combining the distilled water and lye granules. *Always pour the lye into the distilled water and not the other way around, to avoid a mini volcano in your kitchen!* Throughout the rest of the book, this is referred to as lye water.

Although the oils you use determine the way the soap treats your skin, how well it lathers and how moisturizing it is, you may want to experiment with other additives to stir up your senses. Add fragrances, colorants and other additives to your soap and pamper yourself!

Fragrances come in a variety of strengths and scents. Use fragrance and essential oils that are 100% fragrance, so they withstand the soapmaking process.

Fragrances

One way to personalize your bars of soap is to add fragrances by blending essential oils. Before you begin, there are some important things to consider when you add fragrances to your soap.

What Are Essential Oils?

Essential oils are natural plant extracts, which explains why they can be so costly. It also explains why their fragrance varies from brand to brand. Essential oils may smell differently depending on where they are grown and the process by which the oils are extracted. Some oils go through a pressing process whereas other oils are distilled from the plant itself.

Remember that essential oils are extremely powerful, and you should be very cautious when using them. They provide a concentrated amount of fragrance. Using 1½ ounces (45ml) per recipe is plenty.

Some health care professionals advocate that essential oils contribute to patients healing better. While this is debatable, essential and fragrance oils can stimulate a person to recall a memory or lift the spirit. In soapmaking, essential oils add fragrance and invigorate the senses.

What Is the Difference Between Essential Oils and Fragrance Oils?

Fragrance oils are a synthetic version of a scent. They are cheaper than essential oils and more user-friendly to people with plant allergies. Some fragrance oils withstand the soapmaking process better than their essential oil counterparts. Orange is one such example. Sweet orange essential oil is extracted from the meat of the fruit and dissipates very easily. Orange-scented fragrance oils maintain their scent better in the soapmaking process.

Where Do I Find Essential and Fragrance Oils?

You can find essential and fragrance oils in some health stores or aromatherapy stores. You can also order them from soapmaking suppliers, which are usually cheaper. Also consider that most of the essential and fragrance oils available in health food stores are for aromatherapy or massage and will not hold up in a soap recipe. These fragrance oils are diluted in a carrier oil such as almond oil or grapeseed oil. It may become too diluted during the soapmaking process to even detect the scent in your bars of soap. Instead I recommend you use fragrance and essential oils that are 100% pure fragrance. Refer to the Resources section on pages 122–124 in this book to find reasonably priced suppliers of quality soapmaking oils.

Working With Your Fragrance Oil Vendor

When you purchase essential and fragrance oils, it is important to talk to the vendor. Communicate very clearly what you want the oil to smell like. Ask to sample fragrances before you buy them.

Fragrance oils and essential oils are not the same, and they do not smell the same. For instance, lavender essential oil has an earthy scent while the fragrance oil has a sweeter aroma. Peppermint also varies greatly depending on whether you choose the essential oil or the fragrance oil. Sometimes peppermint will have a more medicinal scent and other times it will smell like candy. I suggest you initially purchase smaller quantities as you test which brands and scents work best for you.

Salvaging Soap With Uniscent Fragrance

Because soapmaking is a chemical reaction, it is often difficult to predict how fragrances, colorants and additives will be affected by the saponification process. When adding colorants to your recipe, you may get a completely opposite color than you initially expected. Therefore, it is a good idea to have a "uniscent" fragrance, like wildflowers, handy for those times when the color of the soap does not come out as anticipated. Some pigments are not heat stable or the lye may chemically react with it, thus changing the color. If you are planning on making lavender soap, even if you added a violet colorant, you may get pink soap. Uniscent fragrances are a great way to save a batch of soap should the process alter the color you initially planned.

Blending Essential Oils

Think about when you go to the perfume counter. You try some perfume and initially it may smell sweet and fruity. A little while later, you notice the fragrance has died down to a more subtle scent. A few hours later, you notice the fragrance has now taken on a more floral, earthy scent.

These different characteristic fragrances are called notes. Top notes are generally tart, fruity and light while base notes are more earthy and pungent. Middle notes fall somewhere in between. Top notes seem to disappear completely, but some trace elements remain to complete the fragrance. Base notes help to anchor the top notes. Middle notes help to determine which way the fragrance will lean. Do you prefer flowery? Woodsy? Fruity? The important thing to remember is that you want to balance the top, middle and base notes to create a wonderfully fresh yet not overpowering fragrance.

When blending essential oils, keep this basic formula in mind: three parts top note, two parts middle note and one part base note. This does not mean you have to use six different fragrances when you are blending essential oils. It simply refers to the amount of top note, middle note and base note compared to the total amount of fragrance.

For instance, you may use only one or two fragrance oils for each note. If you really want an orange scent to stand out, for example, you could use sweet orange essential oil for the three top notes, bitter orange for the middle notes and patchouli for the base note. Experiment on your own when blending essential oils. One way to test your combination is to drop some oils on a cotton ball and put it inside a glass jar. Leave it alone for a day and then come back to it.

Common Essential Oils

The following are some of the more common essential oils and their characteristics. For a more comprehensive listing of essential oils, refer to pages 114–119 in the Charts & References Section.

• clary sage
This oil is very earthy and herbaceous. It is excellent as a base note but too overpowering to be used on its own. Blend with mint or citrus oils and use only in small amounts.

• lavender
Lavender is a wonderful fragrance that promotes healing. It is also good for preventative skin care and is often used with tea tree oil. Sample a variety of lavender essential oils before choosing your scent. Lavender can smell vastly different depending on the region where the plant was grown.

• lemongrass
A popular essential oil when soapmaking, lemongrass has a strong citrus scent, but it can also have a medicinal smell. Be sure to sample different varieties before purchasing.

• patchouli
Patchouli is a strong base note with a very earthy smell. Always blend other oils with patchouli. Also, be sure to sample a variety of patchouli fragrances before you buy them.

• peppermint
Peppermint is a revitalizing scent, used to stimulate, rejuvenate and soothe tired muscles. A terpeneless peppermint oil is less likely to cause skin irritations. Sample a variety of peppermint oils. They range from sweet to medicinal.

• petitgrain
This essential oil has a citrus scent. It is commonly used with sweet orange to help the citrus note linger.

• rosemary
Rosemary is often use in soaps because it is slightly antiseptic, making it good for oily skin. It has a sharp herbal scent and is an excellent middle note.

• siberian fir
This is a wonderfully fresh, evergreen scent. It smells like a Christmas tree and is great for making a batch of soap for the holidays.

• sweet orange
This is a very light top note. It is difficult to maintain the scent in soapmaking because it dissipates easily, so you need to use a considerable amount [approximately 1 ounce (30ml)].

Colorants visually complement the recipe and fragrance of the soap.

Color Additives

While color additives are not necessary, it is fun to color your soap. Oxides, ultramarines and food, drug and cosmetic (FD&C) colorants are the color additives most often used in soapmaking. Oxides are heat stable, while ultramarines have a greater range of color to choose from. You can even add natural colorants to your soap with kitchen items.

Natural Colorants

You may want to use natural spices to color your soap. Be cautious with peppery spices, as they may cause skin irritations. Depending on the intensity of the color you want to achieve, use anywhere between ¼–½ tablespoon (4ml–8ml) per 16 ounces (500g) of soap of the following ingredients:

• cocoa powder and cinnamon
These ingredients give your soap a brown tone.

• paprika
Paprika can give your soap an orange color. Do not use hot paprika.

• parsley
Soak fresh parsley in lye water to produce a pale green soap.

• turmeric
This spice produces a mustard shade.

Oxides

Oxides are inorganic color additives, available in green, black, brown, orange, yellow, red and white. Make sure the oxides you buy are cosmetic grade. They are my preferred colorant because they are heat stable and won't react with the lye. You only need to use between ⅟₁₆–¼ teaspoon (0.3ml–1ml) of oxide colorant. Oxides will dry darker than you see them, so it is not necessary to add much at all. While oxides are great because they are heat stable, if you want a wider range of colors, you will need to try other types of color additives. Add oxides when your oils and lye water are tracing.

Ultramarines and Pigments

These colorants can be organic or inorganic and are available in a wide range of colors, but they are less predictable than oxides because they are not heat stable. Sometimes ultramarines will change color throughout the cooking process; other times, the colorant will disappear altogether.

Another problem with ultramarines and pigments is it may be difficult to get a consistent color throughout your batch. They are powders that have to be mixed with small amounts of a carrier oil, like almond or apricot kernel. Add 1 tablespoon (15ml) per batch of soap after the soap mixture has gone through saponification and cooled down a bit for a little more predictability.

FD&C Colorants

Food, drug and cosmetic color additives are organic and another way to color your soap. The advantage of these colorants is they are heat stable; however, they will change color throughout the cooking process. Add no more than ⅛ teaspoon (0.6ml) at trace. It will react with the lye and produce a beautiful color, even if it is a surprise! FD&C colorants can bleed onto washcloths if you add too much, so start out with a small amount and add to it, if necessary.

Natural Additives

Additives are used to give texture as well as enhance the quality of your soap. Some soapmakers like to add fruit to their recipes, but I recommend only adding dried nonperishable materials to your recipe. You can find these additives at grocery stores in your area. Grind them up finely in a coffee grinder and add to your recipe after saponification.

Many kitchen items, such as dried herbs, fresh parsley, honey, oatmeal and powdered goat milk, can enhance your soaps.

• **aloe vera juice**
Use the juice in place of distilled water to give the soap more soothing and healing properties.

• **calendula petals**
Calendula petals will maintain their yellow color throughout the soapmaking process. Soak ¾ cup (180ml) of petals in a lightweight oil, like apricot kernel, and add to your recipe after the soap has saponified.

• **dried herbs**
Using dried herbs like lavender and chamomile is a nice way to add texture to your soap. However, they will turn brown. Lightly coat ¼–½ cup (60ml–120ml) of herbs with a light oil, like almond oil, before adding them after saponification.

• **herbal teas**
Steep three herbal tea bags per 20 ounces (600ml) of distilled water. When the tea has are cooled, combine with lye and go through the rest of the soapmaking process.

• **honey**
Honey is a natural skin softener. When you use 1 tablespoon (15ml) per recipe, you will increase the soap's lather.

• **loofah sponge**
For an exfoliating bar of soap, cut a loofah sponge into ¾" (2cm) squares and lay it in the middle of a flat box mold. Pour the soap mixture into the mold around the loofah.

• **oatmeal**
Oatmeal is a natural exfoliant that soothes dry skin. Use approximately ½ cup (120ml) in a recipe. Don't chop the oats up too finely or you may get soggy soap.

• **parsley**
Add ¼ cup (60ml) of finely chopped parsley to your soap recipe to add green specks to your soap. It will stay green throughout the cook.

• **powdered goat milk**
Adding goat milk to a soap recipe makes a creamy bar of soap. To make a 100% goat milk soap, add 2 tablespoons (30ml) of powdered goat milk for every 8 ounces (237ml) of water in a recipe. See page 46 for instructions on making milk soaps.

• **poppy seeds**
Poppy seeds are a natural exfoliant and add texture to your recipes. Add ¼ cup (60ml) after saponification.

• **pumice**
Add approximately ¼ cup (60ml) of finely ground pumice to your recipe to create an excellent exfoliating soap.

• **salt**
Salt helps to harden the soap. Don't use more than 1 tablespoon (15ml) per recipe because it may make your skin too dry.

• **sugar**
Add approximately 1 tablespoon (15ml) of sugar when combining the distilled water and lye. Sugar will increase the suds of your soap.

Before you begin making soap, be sure you have all of the necessary equipment and materials. You may already have most of these items in your kitchen. You may use the same pots and equipment you cook with—after all, the end result in hot-process soapmaking is soap; lye is no longer present. However, if you prefer to have a separate set, look for these items at a thrift store or yard sale.

Many of the items and equipment necessary for soapmaking can be found in your kitchen.

Cookware

Depending on the method of hot-process soapmaking you prefer, you will need either a slow cooker, a large roaster or a double boiler. When selecting cookware, you can make soap with glass, enamel or stainless steel. While enamel is cheaper, it is also prone to chipping. Once the aluminum is exposed, it can no longer be used for soapmaking because the lye corrodes the aluminum. Stainless steel is the best option because it is lightweight and durable. When sizing your cookware, remember that it should be twice the size of the recipe so the soap mixture will be less likely to boil over.

Slow Cooker

When using a slow cooker to make the recipes in this book, make sure it measures 5–6 quarts (5–6 liters) and has a low-heat setting. Keep in mind that all slow cookers heat differently, and the length of time the soap cooks may differ.

Large Roaster

I recommend a large roaster pan or turkey roaster when making soap in the oven because the short, wide pot allows more surface area for heat to escape. Also, many roasters have lids with vents. When making soap in the oven, make sure heat circulates freely. Lids with vents help the heat escape from inside the roaster. If you do not have a roaster, you may use any large pot that fits in your oven.

Double Boiler

When making soap on your stovetop, you will need a double boiler. The outside pot is filled with boiling water, and it heats the soap in the inside pot. If you do not have a double boiler, you can make one with two pots. It is important that the inside pot is not made of aluminum. With a makeshift double boiler, keep 1"–1½" (3cm–4cm) of space for water between the inside and outside pot. It is important that the water boils freely in the larger pot to keep the heat constant, so the soap can cook uniformly. It is only necessary to have a lid for the inside pot, and I recommend a glass lid so you can see if the soap rises.

Enamel or Stainless Steel Pot

When making soap, you will most likely use recipes that call for solid oils and liquid oils. In order to make a consistent batch of soap, you will need to melt the solid oils and then combine them with the liquid oils. For melting these solid oils, you will need either a small enamel or stainless steel pot.

Digital Scale

While you can create your own makeshift double boiler, you certainly don't want to cut any corners with your scale. Be sure to buy a digital postal scale, available locally at office supply stores or through soapmaking suppliers, that measures to the tenth decimal place. It is also important that the scale have a tare button. Tare refers to the deduction of the weight of the container when taking a measurement. For instance, when you measure out an oil, you must first place the measuring cup on the scale. Push the tare button. The scale will clear and return to zero. If you do not tare the scale, you will not have an accurate measurement, because the scale will weigh both the container and the ingredient. Soapmaking requires careful measurements of oils, water and lye, and a digital scale is the most accurate way to measure out your ingredients.

Stick Blender

An electric stick blender is a convenience tool. You can usually find these small appliances at home stores or yard sales. It has a long handle with a rotating stainless steel blade, which makes combining the oils and lye water much easier than hand stirring. Generally speaking, your soap mixture will begin to trace within approximately 5 minutes.

Glass and Plastic Measuring Cups

When making soap, have glass and plastic measuring cups on hand in various sizes. You will not need to use them for measuring, as you will take all of your measurements with the digital scale, but they are useful because they have a pouring spout and handle. When measuring lye, be sure to always use glass measuring cups because lye crystals cling to plastic cups.

Small Glass Bowls

You may also use small 4–6 ounce (118ml–177ml) glass bowls to take smaller measurements, like measuring fragrance oils, for example.

Long-Handled Plastic Spoon

This is the plastic equivalent of a wooden spoon. It is very important to have a long-handled spoon when making soap to keep your hands away from active lye and heated oils.

Rubber Spatula

With any soap recipe, use a rubber spatula to scrape the inside of the pot or bowl you are using so your measurements are accurate and you do not waste ingredients.

Rubber Mallet and Metal Ice Cream Spade

Some solid oils like palm kernel are difficult to work with. You will need a rubber mallet and a metal ice cream spade to break the solid oil into small manageable pieces.

Funnel

A funnel is helpful when you are filling molds with soap. It saves time and prevents a mess.

Pail Opener

A pail opener is used to open larger containers of oil bought from oil suppliers. It is available at your local hardware store.

STICK BLENDING VS. HAND STIRRING TO TRACE

If you do not have a stick blender, you can stir by hand, but keep in mind, it will take longer. How long you hand stir depends on your recipe. For instance, Spanish castile soap takes approximately 10 minutes to stick blend. Hand stirring takes about 2 hours.

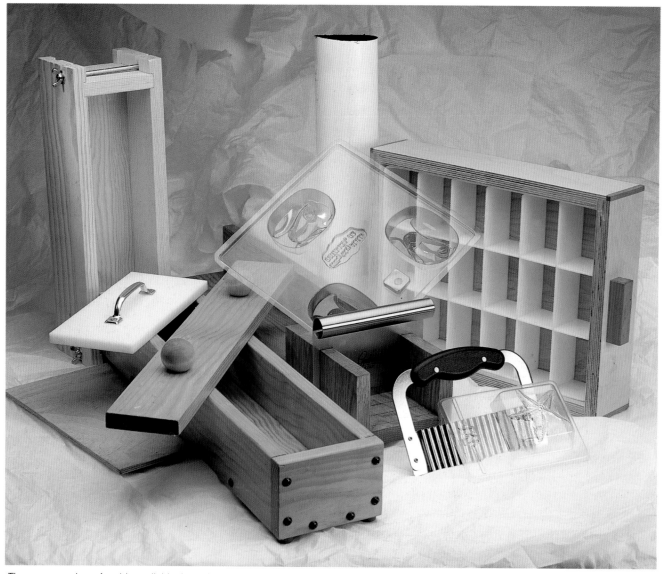

There are a variety of molds available through soapmaking suppliers, as well as some molds you can find in your own kitchen.

Molds

You may think molds are the hardest item to find for soap-making. Actually, a mold is probably the easiest. If you have an old box and freezer paper, you have a mold. All you need to make a mold is a sturdy item that can be either lined with freezer paper or sprayed with an oil spray. Molds are as abundant as your imagination. Just look around.

For the more industrious soapmaker, you may consider buying molds from a soapmaking supplier. There is a wide variety of molds available. Some are made out of plastic and others are made out of wood. Some molds produce traditional bars, but for unique shapes, use plastic cavity molds. See the Resources section on pages 122-124 for mold suppliers. Some of the molds featured in this book include the following:

Plastic Cavity Molds

Plastic cavity molds come in a wide range of shapes and sizes. You can find molds of shapes, flowers, animals, as well as intricate designs. For instance, with the Romantic Rose Soap recipe listed on page 80, you can use a heart shaped mold. Soaps molded from plastic cavity molds make wonderful theme gifts.

Log Mold

If you want to make regular bars of soap, a log mold is an excellent choice. I prefer log molds made of wood that have been specially treated with a plastic-coated varnish. Log molds are perfect for getting uniformly-sized soap. Once the soap has hardened, you can easily slice the log into bars of soap.

Box Mold

A box mold with slats is another way to make bars of soap. Essentially, it is a wooden box with plastic slats that fit together accordingly. Once the soap has saponified, simply pour the soap into the mold and then add the plastic slats to separate each individual bar of soap.

Miscellaneous Supplies

Here are some necessary supplies that make molding your soap that much easier. For more complete instructions on the proper way to fill your molds with soap, refer to pages 48–55.

Freezer Paper and Plastic Trash Bags

To prevent sticking, line the inside of the molds with freezer paper. The shiny plastic coating will prevent the soap from sticking and help you lift out the hardened soap.

Olive Oil Spray

When using a plastic mold, be sure to spray the surface with olive oil or another non-stick spray. This prevents sticking and ensures easy removal from the mold.

Leveler or Trowel

A leveler or a trowel is helpful with log molds and box molds. It evens out the surface of the soap, which decreases the waste when trimming your bars of soap.

✹

Make Your Own Molds

It is simple to make your own molds with items you have around your house. Keep the following things in mind:

1. Make sure it is durable enough to handle hot temperatures and flexible enough to remove the soap once it has hardened.

2. A mold should not be too shallow or too deep. You want to ensure that you can remove the hardened soap easily.

3. Nearly anything plastic can be used for soap molding. Recycle plastic containers and make your own molds.

4. The following kitchen and household items make excellent molds:

- Candy molds

- Gelatin containers

- Heavy cardboard box lined with freezer paper

- Microwavable containers

- Plastic cylinders that carry powdered drinks

- Plastic drawer organizers

- PVC drain pipes

Safety Precautions

You may have all of the ingredients, equipment and supplies, but you are not quite ready to make handcrafted soap. It is extremely important to take the necessary safety measures, including wearing the appropriate safety equipment and knowing what to do in case something unexpected happens. This section will give you the information you need to work carefully. No matter how much experience you have in soapmaking, you can never be too careful or too prepared.

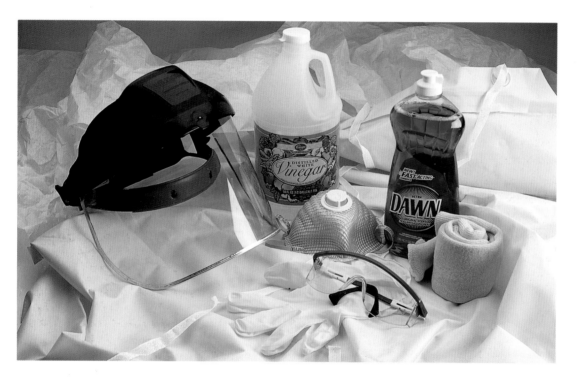

Follow safety precautions every time you make a batch of soap.

Safety Equipment

Before you begin making soap, make sure you have all the important safety equipment.

Protective Clothing

Wear long sleeves, pants and athletic shoes while you make soap. Lye crystals are small and lightweight, and they can easily burn any exposed skin.

Disposable Plastic Gloves

Instead of bulky rubber kitchen gloves, I recommend disposable plastic gloves because they fit snugly and are inexpensive. You can find them at your local pharmacy or discount store.

Plastic Apron

You may want to wear a plastic apron to protect your clothing. They are inexpensive and reusable.

Arm Protectors

Breathable arm protectors are optional, but recommended, especially in the summertime. You can find them at any soapmaking supplier. An alternative to wearing arm protectors is to simply wear a long-sleeved shirt, but the arm protectors are preferred because they are form-fitting.

Safety Glasses

The most important safety precaution is eye protection. No matter how comfortable you become with soapmaking, never

24

handle lye without safety glasses. Lye crystals are so small and can be very damaging to your eyes. Protect your eyes with safety glasses found at your local hardware store. Make sure they fit comfortably and do not slip.

Face Shield

You may also consider buying a face shield from a hardware store or an industrial safety supplier. Not only does a face shield cover your eyes, it also protects your entire face.

Ventilation Mask

Because of the fumes caused by combining water and lye, you may want to wear a ventilation mask. You should always combine the water and lye in a well-ventilated area, but this mask offers added protection. They are available at hardware stores.

Lye Precautions

If your skin comes into contact with lye, it will begin to itch. Then it will begin to burn. Wash the affected area with a soapy vinegar mixture. To make this mixture, fill a measuring cup with equal parts of soapy water and white vinegar. Vinegar is a weak acid, whereas lye is an alkali (or base). The soapy vinegar mixture will neutralize the lye. Use this mixture to rinse off utensils and measuring cups that have come in contact with the lye. Also, keep this mixture close by in case your skin comes in contact with the lye. Note: If you happen to get lye or lye water in your eye, rinse out your eye with water for fifteen minutes. Then call your doctor immediately.

Splashing

Splashing lye water or your soap mixture can cause irritation or burns. Here are some practical ways to avoid common mistakes.

1. Oversize the Equipment

Whether you are using measuring cups, your slow cooker, double boiler or large roaster, always overestimate the size of the batch of soap you are making. As a general rule of thumb, your equipment should hold twice as much soap as you actually need. When working with lye and heated oils, burns can be severe. Exercise caution.

2. Keep Your Stick Blender Under the Surface of the Soap

When using your stick blender to reach trace, it is very easy to lift the blade above the soap surface, causing you to splash the soap mixture. Keep the stick blender under the surface to avoid accidents.

3. Pour Facing Away From You

When adding the lye water to your oils, always pour slowly away from you. If it should splash out of your soap pot, it will not splash out and cause you harm.

✳

How to Prevent Your Soap Mixture From Boiling Over

Because heating elements like stoves, ovens and slow cookers vary in intensity and amount of heat they produce, you will get a feel for how your equipment works the more you use. Be aware of your ingredients and equipment to avoid soap from boiling over out of your pot. While the soap cooks, be very cautious of what is going on. Keep the following factors in mind:

- YOUR INGREDIENTS. Remember, animal fats heat up hotter than vegetable oils.

- YOUR RECIPE. How large is the batch of soap you are making? Remember that all of your equipment, from measuring cups to the pot you are cooking the soap in, can hold twice the size of the yield of the recipe.

- YOUR POT. Does the lid have a vent to allow heat to escape? Is your pot made of stainless steel, enamel or glass? They all have various weights and heat up differently. Keep a close watch on your pot and never leave your soap unattended as it cooks.

- YOUR INDIVIDUAL SET-UP. Be aware of how much surface area there is for pent up heat to escape. A tall thin pot will heat up faster and hotter than a shorter and wider pot because there is less surface area. A tall thin pot is therefore more likely to boil over.

methods

There are many ways to make soap, from cold process to hot process, on a stove, in an oven or even in a slow cooker. Some people prefer to make soap in a pot, using the direct heat from a stove, whereas others even use a microwave. The following methods in this book are all hot-process methods using an indirect heat source. This means the pot of soap does not come into direct contact with the heating element. Even if you have never attempted soapmaking before, you can follow these simple instructions and easily make wonderful bars of soap that your skin will love.

The hot-process method is the easiest and most convenient way to make soap. You can literally make the soap during the day and shower with it that same night! It is that simple. You can make hot-process soap using one of the three following methods: slow cooker, oven and double boiler. You may find you prefer one method over the other two. Pick the method that works best for you, and in no time you will be able to pamper yourself and your family and friends with handcrafted soap you made yourself.

Including:

This is the easiest of all the hot-process soapmaking methods when done correctly. Use a slow cooker that has a lift-out bowl, and make sure the outer section of the cooker uniformly heats the bowl. For faster soapmaking, preheat the slow cooker for 10 minutes and cook the soap on the lowest setting. It takes an average of 45–60 minutes before you can add the soap into the molds.

Materials

- slow cooker
- enamel or stainless steel pot
- digital scale
- stick blender
- 64-ounce (2L), 32-ounce (960ml) and 16-ounce (480ml) plastic and glass measuring cups
- small glass bowls
- stainless steel measuring spoon (optional)
- rubber spatula
- long-handled plastic spoon
- rubber mallet
- metal ice cream spade
- soapy vinegar mixture (see page 25)
- safety equipment

TIP
· · · · ·
Use glass or stainless steel containers when measuring lye granules because they cling to plastic containers.

1 **Measure the Distilled Water and Lye**
Place a 32-ounce (960ml) measuring cup on the scale and tare to zero. Measure the correct amount of distilled water. Next, place a 16-ounce (480ml) measuring cup on the scale. Again, tare the scale to zero. Measure out the correct amount of lye. When you get close to the amount needed, shake a few granules at a time to prevent overpouring. If you do overpour, simply lift out some of the crystals with a stainless steel tablespoon, and sprinkle them back in until you get the correct measurement. Slowly place the excess crystals back into the lye container.

2 Combine Water and Lye

In a well-ventilated area, carefully pour the lye into the distilled water while slowly stirring with a long-handled plastic spoon. Take the necessary safety precautions and wear protective clothing, safety glasses and a ventilation mask. I recommend working beneath a stove vent that has a strong suction to pull the fumes upward. Stir until you are certain all the lye crystals have dissolved. Set aside, out of the way of children, pets or the possibility of being knocked over.

3 Neutralize Any Leftover Lye Crystals

Immediately after you have combined the lye and distilled water, neutralize the lye residue in the glass measuring cup and on the long-handled plastic spoon by pouring the soapy vinegar mixture over them.

4 Preheat the Slow Cooker and Break Up the Solid Oils

Preheat for your slow cooker for 10 minutes. While it is heating up, break up the solid oils with a rubber mallet and a metal ice cream spade.

5 Measure the Solid Oils

Place your enamel or stainless steel pot on the digital scale and tare the scale to zero. Measure out your solid oils, and each time tare the scale to ensure correct measurements. Since many solid oils look alike, I suggest you start at the top of the recipe and work your way down in order to help you keep track.

6 Melt the Solid Oils

When all of the solid oils are measured, place the enamel or stainless steel pot on a low-heat burner and begin melting the solid oils.

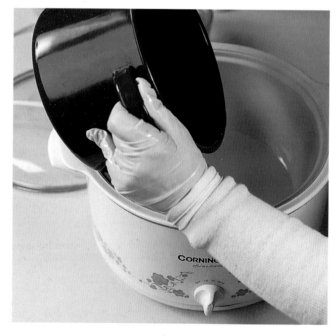

7 Add Melted Solid Oils to the Slow Cooker

Once the solid oils have melted, slowly pour them into the preheated slow cooker. Pour slowly and carefully; you may even want to face the pouring side away from you. Use a rubber spatula to scrape the excess oil out of the heated pot.

8 Measure the Liquid Oils

Tare to zero and measure out all of your liquid oils. Remember that oils have different weights. Heavier oils will not pour as much volume into the cup as lighter oils. If you prefer, you can measure all of the oils out into separate measuring cups, or you may combine them all together in one larger measuring cup.

9 Add the Liquid Oils

Pour the liquid oils into the slow cooker while stirring with a long-handled plastic spoon or rubber spatula. Maintain the cooker on a low heat setting. This is especially important when using a recipe that calls for items that quickly heat up to high temperatures, such as lard, tallow, beeswax and jojoba.

10 Add the Lye Water

Slowly pour the lye water into the slow cooker and mix with a stick blender. Remember to always keep the blade of the stick blender below the surface of the soap mixture so it does not accidentally splash you. At this point add any oxide, FD&C or natural color additives to your recipe. Remember, ultramarines are added after the cook.

11 **Blend the Soap Mixture**

Continue to slowly move the stick blender around the slow cooker. As you blend the oils, distilled water and lye, saponification will begin. It takes about 5 minutes to bring a mixture to trace. You will notice the mixture begin to thicken.

12 **Continue to Blend**

Continue to stick blend until the mixture resembles instant pudding. As you move your blender around the soap mixture, you may find that the stick blender creates a suction to the bottom of the slow cooker. If this should occur, turn off the blender then tilt it off the bottom of the cooker. If you mix while tilting the blender at a very slight angle, you will not have the suction problem.

13 **Cook for an Hour**

Place the lid on the slow cooker and relax nearby for the next 45–60 minutes. Watch through the glass lid as the soap mixture changes. If you have a lid that is not very transparent, lift the lid quickly for a peek every 15 minutes. Do not keep the lid off longer than about 5 seconds or you may lose too much heat and slow the cooking process. You will notice the soap goes through many changes as it cooks. First, the soap will seem to thicken even more in the center of the slow cooker and smooth out a bit. The edges touching the cooker will rise a bit and curl toward the center, looking like waves, while the center is still smooth and solid. Therefore, this stage is called the "waves and island".

14 **Soap Continues Cooking Through Saponification**

As the soap continues to cook, the waves will roll closer toward the center, making the island smaller. When the island has sunk beneath the waves, you will see liquid floating on top of what now is somewhat transparent in consistency. This liquid is the natural glycerin that saponified from the oils, distilled water and lye. Stir the glycerin back into the soap.

15 **Remove Soap From Heat**
Turn the slow cooker off. Lift the bowl out of the heating element. Stir to cool down the soap mixture as if you were folding ingredients into a cake mixture, lifting from the center to open it up. This will help release the internal heat from the soap and cool the mixture more evenly than if you let it sit.

16 **Measure the Fragrance Oil**
Place a small glass bowl on the scale and tare it to zero. Slowly and carefully add the fragrance or essential oils of your choice. The fragrance and the potency is entirely up to you. I like strongly scented soaps, so I use 1 ounce (30ml) of fragrance per pound (454g) of soap. Use less if you are using essential oils or strong fragrances.

17 **Add Fragrance to the Soap Mixture**
Add the fragrance to the soap mixture, stirring well to ensure even consistency throughout the mixture.

➤ *To put the soap into molds and finish the soap-making process, refer to the molds section on pages 48–55.*

A large roaster is the ideal way to make hot-process soap using the oven method. The roaster should be wide, so heat doesn't build up. It should also be low enough to help prevent burning your arms while pulling it out of a hot oven. I recommend a stainless steel roaster with a vent in the lid. If you do not have a large roaster, you can still make soap using the oven method by using any large pot. The advantage to making soap using the oven method is you can make a fairly large batch of soap in a short amount of time.

Materials

- large roaster or pot
- enamel or stainless steel pot
- digital scale
- stick blender
- 64-ounce (2L), 32-ounce (960ml) and 16-ounce (480ml) plastic and glass measuring cups
- small glass bowls
- stainless steel measuring spoon (optional)
- rubber spatula
- long-handled plastic spoon
- rubber mallet
- metal ice cream spade
- aluminum foil
- soapy vinegar mixture (see page 25)
- safety equipment

TIP

Use glass or stainless steel containers when measuring lye granules because they cling to plastic containers.

1 **Measure the Distilled Water and Lye**

Place the plastic measuring cup on the scale and tare the scale to zero. Measure the correct amount of distilled water according to your recipe. In a glass measuring cup, measure the correct amount of lye. If you happen to overpour the lye, simply remove the excess with a stainless steel tablespoon.

2 Combine the Distilled Water and Lye

In a well-ventilated area, pour the lye into the distilled water while slowly stirring with a long-handled plastic spoon. Always pour the lye into the distilled water and not the other way around.

3 Neutralize Any Leftover Lye Crystals

Immediately after you have combined the lye and distilled water, neutralize any remaining lye crystals on the glass measuring cup and the plastic spoon by pouring the soapy vinegar mixture over them.

4 Break Up Solid Oils

Begin to break up some of your solid oils with a rubber mallet and metal ice cream spade, if necessary.

5   Preheat the Oven

Line the bottom rack in your oven completely with aluminum foil, and preheat your oven to 180°–200° F (82°–93° C).

6   Measure the Solid Oils

Place the enamel or stainless steel pot on your digital scale, tare the scale to zero and add your first solid oil. Add each of the remaining solid oils and remember to tare the scale between each measurement. Since many solid oils look alike, start at the top of the recipe and work your way down. Once all of the solid oils are measured, melt them on low heat on your stove.

7 **Measure the Liquid Oils**

Place your 64-ounce (2L) glass measuring cup on the scale and tare to zero. If you choose to measure out all of your liquid oils into the measuring cup, remember to tare the scale between each measurement. Be aware that oils have different weights. Heavier oils will not pour as much volume into the cup as lighter-weight oils. Therefore, don't try to eyeball the amount. Accidentally overpouring by a fraction of an ounce generally will not present a problem in a recipe, but more than that may cause a noticeable softening of your soap, and it will take longer to harden.

8 **Gather Melted Solid Oils, Liquid Oils and Lye Water**

By the time you finish measuring the liquid oils, the solid oils should be melted. Remove the melted oils from the heat and carefully combine the oils together in the large roaster. Pour the oils facing away from you to avoid accidental burns. Remember, oils heat up hotter than water, and the burns can be much more severe. Use a rubber spatula to scrape the remaining oil out of the pot.

9 **Add Lye Water to Oils**

Slowly pour the lye water into the large roaster with the oils as you mix with your stick blender. Always keep the blade of the stick blender below the surface of the mixture so soap does not accidentally splash out. Continue to move the stick blender around the roaster, blending the oils, distilled water and lye, reaching trace and starting saponification. This process averages about 5 minutes. It may take longer if you have more solids oils in a recipe. The larger the recipe, the more time it will take to bring it to trace. It will resemble instant pudding as it thickens.

10 Cook the Soap

After you combine the lye water and oils, you may want to add oxide, FD&C or natural colorants to the soap. Oxide color additives will dry darker than you see them, so start with only a pinch of color to begin. If you prefer using ultramarines and pigments, wait until the soap has cooked and slightly cooled. Place a lid on the soap pot. The total cooking time is approximately 30–40 minutes.

11 Check the Soap After 20 Minutes

Every 10 minutes, check on your pot of soap to make sure the soap is not boiling over, by observing the pot through the oven door window. If you do not have an oven window, open the door just far enough to see the pot, but do not allow too much heat to escape. After 20–30 minutes, carefully pull the soap pot out of the oven and visually inspect the soap.

12 Stir to Release Heat

After 30–40 minutes in the oven, the soap should look translucent and shiny with glycerine on top. Carefully remove the roaster from the oven. Be sure you have a good grip before lifting. The pot will be hot and heavy. Stir the soap mixture as if you were folding ingredients into a cake mixture, lifting from the center. This will help release the internal heat from the soap and cool down the mixture faster and more evenly than if you let it sit. The larger the mass of soap, the longer you will need to fold to release heat.

13 Measure the Fragrance Oils

In a small glass bowl, combine any fragrance or essential oils you want to add to the soap recipe. I prefer strongly scented soaps so I use 1 ounce (30 ml) of fragrance per pound (454 ml) of soap. Use less when using essential oils or really strong fragrances.

14 Add Fragrance Oils

Pour fragrance oils into the soap mixture and stir well for uniformity.

> ➤ **FILLING MOLDS**
> *To add soap into molds and finish the soapmaking process, refer to the molds section on pages 48–55.*

Another very simple way to make hot-process soap is right on your stovetop with a double boiler. If you don't have a double boiler, you can easily make one out of two pots. When you use a double boiler, the water in the outside pot heats and cooks the soap in the inside pot. If you do not have a slow cooker or a large roaster, you can still make soap using this quick and easy method.

Materials

- double boiler
- digital scale
- stick blender
- 64-ounce (2L), 32-ounce (960ml) and 16-ounce (480ml) plastic and glass measuring cups
- small glass bowls
- stainless steel measuring spoon (optional)
- rubber spatula
- long-handled plastic spoon
- rubber mallet
- metal ice cream spade
- aluminum foil (if necessary)
- soapy vinegar mixture (see pg. 25)
- safety equipment

TIP

· · · · ·

Use glass or stainless steel containers when measuring lye granules because they cling to plastic containers.

 **Measure the Distilled Water and Lye**
Place the 32-ounce (960ml) plastic or glass measuring cup on the scale and tare the scale to zero. Measure the correct amount of distilled water. Next, place a 16-ounce (480ml) glass measuring cup on the scale. Again tare the scale to zero. Measure out the correct amount of lye. Try not to overpour. If you do, simply scoop the excess crystals out with a stainless steel measuring spoon.

2 Combine the Distilled Water and Lye

In a well-ventilated area, carefully pour the lye into the distilled water while slowly stirring with a long-handled plastic spoon. Work beneath a stove vent that has a strong suction and wear a ventilation mask. Stir until all of the lye crystals have dissolved. Set aside, out of the way, to avoid accidental spills.

3 Neutralize Any Leftover Lye Crystals

Immediately after you have combined the lye and water, neutralize any remaining lye in the glass measuring cup and the long-handled spoon by rinsing them with the soapy vinegar mixture.

4 Preheat Water Pot and Break Up Solid Oils

Fill the outside pot of the double boiler with water and turn the stove on high. The water level should be full enough so that when you add the soap pot inside the water pot, water surrounds the soap completely. When the water begins to boil, turn the heat to low and add the lid on if you are not quite ready to cook the soap. However, once you are ready to cook the soap, make sure the burner is high enough to maintain a gentle rolling boil.

5 Measure the Solid Oils

Place a 64-ounce (2L) glass measuring cup on your scale. Tare the scale to zero. Begin to measure out your solid oils. Add each remaining solid oil and remember to tare the scale between each measurement.

6 Heat the Solid Oils

When all the solid oils are melted, add them to the inside pot of the double boiler. Melt the oils on low heat. Meanwhile, the larger outside pot is still heating up.

7 Measure the Liquid Oils

While the solid oils are heating up, carefully measure the liquid oils. Place your glass measuring cup on the scale and press the tare button so the scale reads zero. Add the liquid oils, one at a time, remembering to tare the scale between each measurement. Accidentally overpouring by a fraction of an ounce generally will not present a problem in a recipe, but more than that may cause noticeable softening of your soap and it will take longer to harden.

8 Combine the Melted and Liquid Oils

Once the solid oils have melted, slowly pour the liquid oils into the soap pot. Pour the oils slowly to avoid splashing. Oils heat hotter than water, so burns can be much more severe. Use a rubber spatula to scrape the excess oil out of the measuring cup and into the soap pot.

9 Add the Lye Water and Color Additives

Slowly pour the lye water into the oils as you mix with your stick blender. At this point, you may want to add oxide colorants or FD&C colors to the soap. If you are using ultramarines, add them after the cook. Remember to always keep the blade of the stick blender below the surface of the soap mixture. Slowly move the stick blender around the pot, blending the oils, distilled water and lye, starting the process of saponification. This process averages 5 minutes. Remember, trace is a thickening of the soap as it begins to saponify. It will resemble instant pudding as it thickens.

10. **Place the Soap Pot Inside the Water Pot**
Once the soap mixture has thickened, carefully put the soap pot into the water pot. The water should be boiling high enough to maintain a gentle rolling boil.

11. **Cook the Soap**
Place a lid on the soap pot only. You want to maintain constant heat, so you may need to put aluminum foil on the outside pot to keep the steam in. Remember you want to have 1"–1½" (3cm–4cm) of space between the soap pot and the water pot.

12. **Measure the Fragrance**
When the soap has nearly saponified, measure out the proper amount of fragrance for your recipe. I like strongly scented soaps, so I use 1 ounce (30 ml) of fragrance per 1 pound (454g) of soap recipe. Use less if you are using essential oils or really strong fragrances. Add any other natural additives at this point as well.

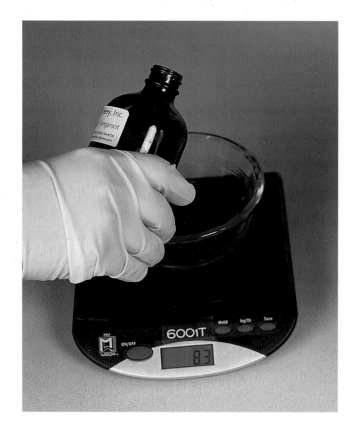

13 Check The Soap Every 15 Minutes

While the soap is cooking, stir it every 15 minutes with a rubber spatula to help redistribute the heat. The soap in the middle of the pot does not heat the same as the soap touching the outside edge. You can see as it cooks, the traced soap looks like applesauce. It will begin to curl a bit around the edges and work its way toward the center of the pot. When you stir it and it does not appear wet, your mixture has either saponified fully or is close to being saponified. To test this, lift your rubber spatula out of the mixture and carefully touch the tip of your pointer finger to a thinly coated area of the spatula. Rub it between your pointer finger and thumb. If it feels gritty, it is not yet saponified. Allow it to cook another 10 minutes and repeat this rubbing test. When the soap smoothly rubs between your fingers and cools rapidly, the soap is finished cooking.

14 Add the Fragrance to the Soap Mixture

Once the soap has fully saponified, carefully remove the soap pot out of the double boiler. Be careful, as the pot will be very hot. Using a rubber spatula, thoroughly stir in the fragrance.

➤ **FILLING MOLDS**
At this point, you are ready to add your soap mixture to the mold of your choice. To finish the soapmaking process, refer to the molds section on pages 48–55.

Milk soap recipes are slightly different than non-milk soap recipes. You can make milk soaps using any of the three hot-process methods with a few additional steps. In addition, you will also need a measuring spoon and a whisk. For a creamy bar of soap, I recommend making Boone's Lather Goat Milk Soap on page 96. Follow these supplementary guidelines when making milk soaps.

1 Measure the Distilled Water

Take out 25% of the distilled water, split it in half and place it into two smaller plastic measuring cups. Place one of the small measuring cups in the freezer and use the second to combine with powdered milk. The remaining 75% of water will be used to combine with the lye.

2 Measure the Powdered Goat's Milk

Carefully measure the powdered milk. To make 100% milk soap, use 2 tablespoons (75ml) of powdered milk for each 8 ounces (240ml) of distilled water in the total recipe.

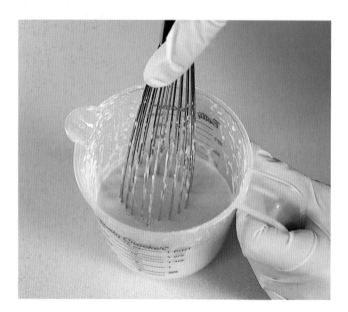

3 Whisk the Powdered Milk and Distilled Water

Whisk the powdered milk in one of the split 25% cups of water until you have a smooth, thick paste that resembles cake batter. Place it in the freezer. Note: Freezer settings may vary. You want the water to begin to get icy, but not to freeze solid. The milk mixture should become a thick paste. Add the lye to the remaining 75% of water and continue the soap recipe as usual and cook through saponification.

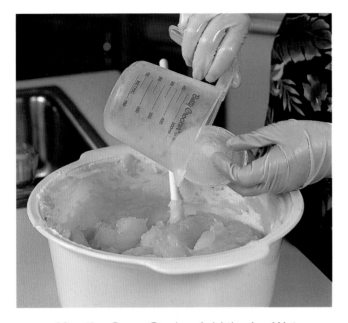

4 After the Soap Cooks, Add the Icy Water

After you remove the soap mixture from heat, stir the mixture to release some of the heat. Then, add the distilled water you placed in the freezer (from step 1). It should not be frozen solid, but icy, and should break up before you stir it into the mixture. You will notice bubbles, but as you stir, they will mix in. Stir rather quickly. You don't want the icy water to stay in one area for very long because it will cause that part of the soap to harden too quickly, resulting in speckled soap. You want to stir quickly enough to maintain uniform cooling. Next, add your fragrance oils to further cool the soap.

5 Add the Fragrance and the Icy Goat Milk

After you have added the fragrance of your choice to the soap mixture, remove the milk mixture from the freezer. It should be a pastelike consistency. Fold the mixture into the soap by lifting from the center to open it up. Using your rubber spatula, scrape all of the paste into the soap mixture and stir well to ensure uniformity. Work quickly because your soap is now cool and will solidify faster than a non-milk soap. You are now ready to mold your soap.

TIP
• • • • •

I do not recommend adding colorants to milk soaps. The heat will caramelize the sugars and turn the soap tan if added before the soap cools sufficiently.

After saponification, you are ready to put the mixture into soap molds to set and harden. After the soap has cooled, it usually takes a couple of hours until it is ready to use. There are a variety of molds you can use from plastic cavity molds to log molds. You can even make your own molds out of common household items. The next few pages show you step-by-step how to fill a variety of molds.

Using a Log Mold

To make rectangular bars of soap, log molds are easy and convenient. They are often made of wood and there are a variety to choose from. Some are treated with a plastic varnish, but I recommend you use freezer paper to line the inside of the mold for easier clean up. You can find log and box molds at soap supply companies both online and in your area. When using a log mold, you will need olive oil spray, freezer paper and a soap miter box and cutter.

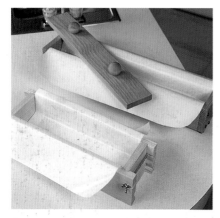

1 **Line the Molds With Freezer Paper**

It is only necessary to line the longer section of the mold. Be sure you have the shiny side up when lining with freezer paper. That side has the plastic coating. With olive oil spray, coat the shorter sides of the mold.

2 **Fill the Mold With Soap**

Use a spoon or spatula to fill the mold. Lift the mold 4" (10cm) off the counter and drop it once or twice. Repeat this filling and tapping process several times until the mold is full of soap. This helps gravity spread out the soap and release air bubbles. Note: If you have a fragile countertop, you may want to tap the mold on the floor.

3 **Press the Lid on the Mold**

The soap may need smoothing out. Spray the top of the soap with olive oil spray and lay the freezer paper and log mold lid on top.

4 Smooth Out the Soap

When the surface of the soap is smooth to your satisfaction, gently peel back the freezer paper.

5 Overfill to Trim Any Excess

If your mold does not have a lid, overfill the mold and allow the soap to dry out for a few hours. When it is dry, trim off any excess with a cutter.

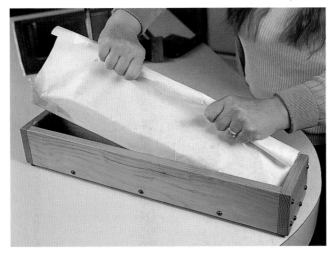

6 Remove Soap From Mold

Once the soap has hardened, carefully pull the soap out of the mold by grasping the freezer paper. Remove and discard the freezer paper.

7 Slice the Soap Into Bars

Slide the molded soap into the cutter. Slice the soap into rectangular bars. Most soaps are approximately ¾"–1" (2–3cm) thick.

Box Mold

A box mold with slats is another way to make rectangular bars of soap. This mold is available at soap supply stores or online. It works the same way an old-fashioned ice cube tray works. In addition to the mold, you will also need a plastic trash bag, wax paper, olive oil spray and a trowel to smooth the top of the soap.

Line the Box

To prevent the soap from sticking to the mold, as well as to cut down on cleanup time, line the mold with a plastic trash bag. Secure the bag with the outer band of the mold. Pull the trash bag tight enough to smooth out the wrinkles. Spray with olive oil spray to avoid sticking.

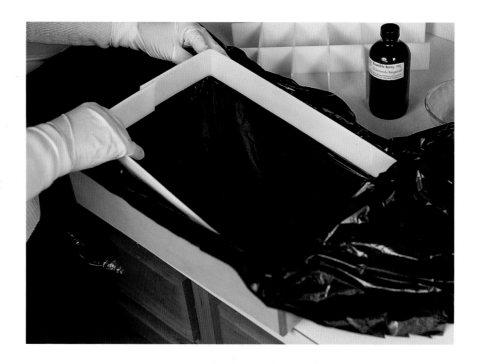

Add the Soap Mixture

Carefully add the soap into the mold using a rubber spatula.

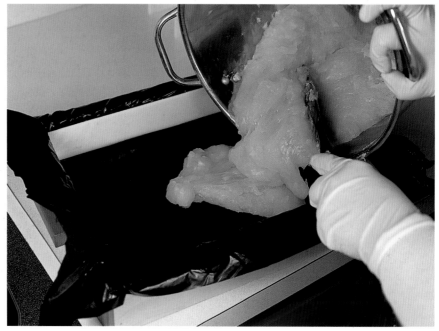

3 Evenly Distribute Soap

Drop the box onto the countertop a few times to remove any air bubbles and evenly distribute the soap. To protect your countertop, place a thick cloth placemat under the mold, or tap the soap on the floor.

4 Coat the Soap

Evenly spray a coating of olive oil onto the top surface of the soap. Cover the soap with wax paper.

5 Smooth Out the Surface

Using a soap trowel, carefully smooth and even out the surface of the soap. Slowly remove the wax paper.

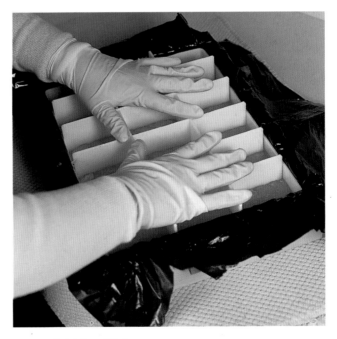

6 Add the Slats

Spray the slats with olive oil and gently press them into the soap mixture. Allow the soap to set. When dry, remove the soap by turning the box upside down. Remove the plastic bag and if the soap seems stuck, push the soap bars through the slats.

Plastic Cavity Molds

Craft stores and online venders offer a wide variety of plastic cavity molds. Experiment and be creative with your soap! For instance, with goat milk soap, use goat's head molds. Plastic cavity molds are a great way to really dress up your soaps. You will need olive oil spray and a cutter along with your molds.

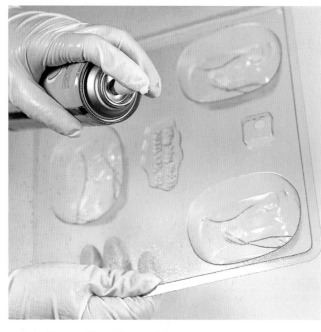

1. Spray the Plastic Molds
Using an olive oil spray, lightly coat the inside of the sheet of cavity molds.

2. Add the Soap
With a long-handled plastic spoon, add enough soap to the molds to cover the intricate design. You do not want to leave any air bubbles that can ruin the design of the mold.

3. Tap the Molds
Gently but firmly, tap the molds on the countertop, ensuring that the soap is evenly distributed. Do this quickly because the soap will harden rather quickly.

4. Trim Any Excess
Once the soap has dried, trim excess soap with a cutter. Remove the soap from the molds and let it continue to harden.

Make Your Own Molds

Instead of going out and buying soap molds, be creative! Look around your house for possible molds recycled from common household items. Anything that is plastic makes a great mold, from drawer organizers to a PVC pipe. The possibilities are endless! In addition to your mold, you will need freezer paper, olive oil spray and a funnel.

Making a PVC Pipe Mold

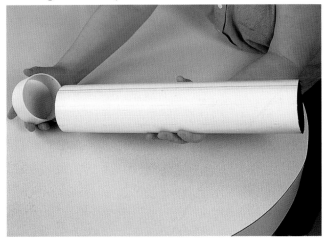

1 Spray Pipe and Cap with Olive Oil
Get a PVC pipe and cap that measures 2" or 3" (5cm or 8cm) in diameter. Spray the cap with olive oil spray and put it on the pipe.

2 Measure the Freezer Paper
Measure and cut the freezer paper and PVC pipe so that the freezer paper is 3" (8cm) longer than the pipe. Freezer paper usually comes in 18" (46cm) rolls, so an ideal length for the PVC pipe is 15" (38cm). Cut the freezer paper, leaving a 1" (3cm) overlap.

3 Insert the Freezer Paper Into the PVC Pipe
Place the freezer paper inside the pipe, shiny side toward the soap. Roll the paper tightly then release it to open after it is inside the pipe and against the cap on the bottom. Spray the freezer paper with olive oil, ensuring that the soap will not stick.

4 Fill the Mold With the Soap Mixture
Spray a funnel with olive oil, and carefully spoon soap into the opening. Every 2"–3" (5cm–8cm) tap the pipe on the countertop to help gravity push the soap down and release air bubbles. Set aside, upright, to harden for 3–4 hours. To remove the soap from the PVC mold, proceed to page 55.

Using a Plastic Container As a Mold

1 **Cut Off the Top of the Plastic Container**

With a sharp knife, remove the rim and lid of the plastic container you are making into a mold. When recycling a empty lye container for a soap mold, be sure to neutralize with soapy vinegar water and rinse well.

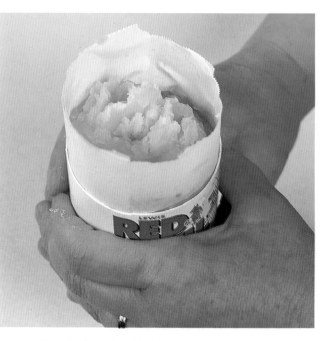

3 **Firmly Tap the Mold**

Once the mold has been halfway filled, firmly tap it on the countertop to remove any air bubbles and evenly distribute the soap. Add more soap to the mold and tap again. Set the mold aside to harden.

2 **Line and Fill the Container**

Line the container with freezer paper, spray with olive oil and fill the container with the soap mixture. Remember to coat the funnel with olive oil as well.

Removing Soap From the Mold

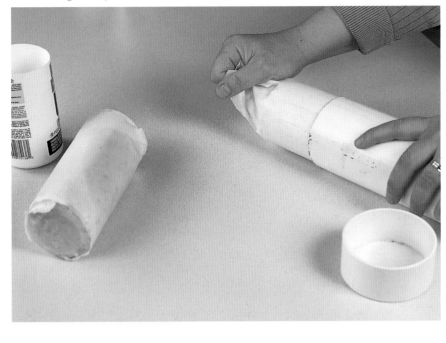

1 Remove the Soap

Once the soap has hardened, remove the cap and pull the soap from the pipe. Once you have removed the soap from the mold, remove and discard the freezer paper.

2 Slice the Molded Soap

Place the molded soap into the miter box. With your cutter, trim off any uneven ends. Using the miter box, slice the soap into bars.

A simple alternative to true soapmaking is the Melt & Pour method. Whereas the hot-process methods you just learned are designed to make luxurious bars of soap, melt & pour soaps are fun if you would like to make multilayered or multicolored decorative soaps. If you have children who want to help make soap and you would like a safer alternative to lye and oils, Melt & Pour is a wonderful activity for you to do together. While you will notice a difference between the Melt & Pour soap and the hot-process soap on your skin, it can be a lot of fun to make!

Materials

- medium-sized double boiler
- block of melt & pour base soap (available at craft stores)
- food coloring or mica
- spray bottle filled with rubbing alcohol
- sharp knife
- plastic mold of your choice
- small glass bowls
- candy sticks (available at craft stores) or plastic spoons
- wax paper
- paring knife

1 Slice the Base Soap

Estimate the amount of base soap you need and slice it into small pieces. The soap already comes in blocks, but it melts faster if you slice it into thin pieces.

2 Melt the Soap

Place the soap pieces in the top pan of a heated double boiler on low to medium heat. The water pot of the double boiler should be boiling.

3 Add Food Coloring

Once the soap has melted, add the food coloring of your choice. Use a candy stick to stir the coloring. Continue stirring until the soap is evenly colored. You may add the coloring in the pan or transfer the base soap into glass bowls to create more than one color at a time.

4 Spray the Colored Soap

Using a spray bottle filled with rubbing alcohol, spray the soap to break up surface tension and release the bubbles that form on the surface.

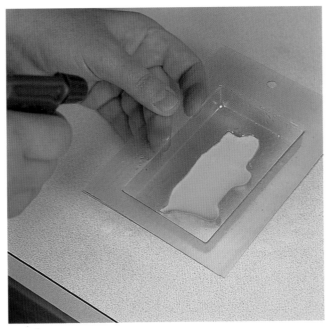

5 Pour Into the Mold of Your Choice

Pour the soap mixture into the mold, being careful not to overfill it. Spray the Melt & Pour soap once again with alcohol after it is in the mold.

6 Let the Soap Set and Form a Skin

In order to make a multilayered, multicolored bar of soap, the soap must develop a skin on the top so the colors do not run together. Some molds, like this pig mold, may not sit flat on a counter. You will need to set these kinds of molds on two identically sized objects to keep them level.

7 Melt the Second Layer of Soap

Slice more base soap and melt it on the stove. Once it has melted, add the coloring either in the double boiler or in a small glass bowl. Spray with alcohol to release surface tension bubbles.

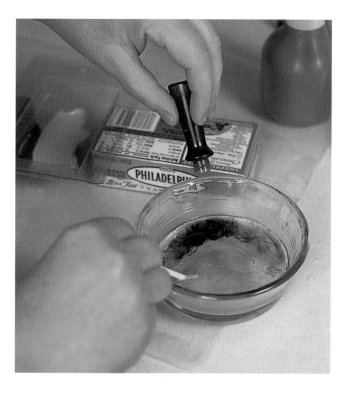

8 Add the Second Soap Layer

Spray the skinned layer to help the new layer adhere, and pour your next soap color into the mold. It is easier to remove the soap from the mold if you leave a ⅛" (0.3cm) space between the soap and the top of the mold.

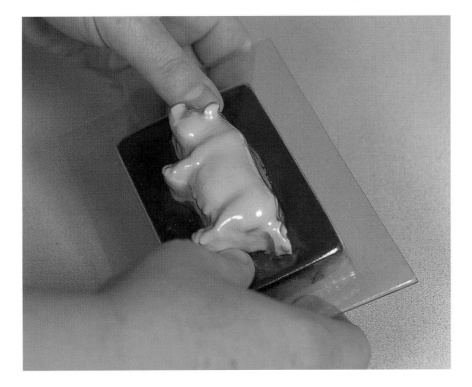

9 **Remove the Soap From the Mold**

When cooled thoroughly, approximately 20 minutes, remove your decorative bar of soap. If it seems stuck, put it in the freezer for about 15 minutes and then remove it.

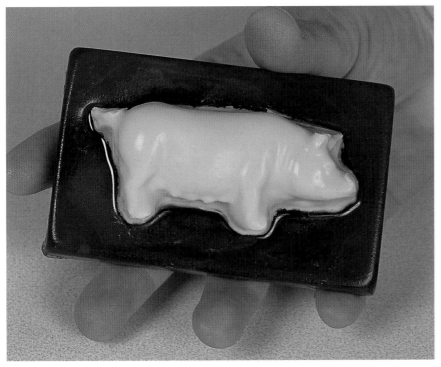

10 **Add Final Touches**

When you are finished, check for any areas where you may have overpoured the mold. If you need to make any corrections, use a paring knife.

recipes

To make true soap you must always use lye, oils and distilled water. There is no changing that. The creative part comes when you personalize your soap. There are many variables—climate, humidity and the altitude where you live; the different oils in your recipe; the cooking methods you use; and the size of your batch of soap—that influence how your batch of soap will turn out.

Your personal preferences will also determine what kind of soap best suits you and your needs. This book includes twenty-eight recipes for you to experiment with and enjoy. You may be the type of person who loves the soothing effects of lavender or chamomile, or you may prefer the refreshing, invigorating scent of citrus. You may have sensitive skin and want a very mild cleanser, free from any synthetic colorants or fragrances. Select a recipe from pages 64–99 and pick one of the three methods that works best for you. You will have a great time making soap, and your skin will love it too!

Including:

Sunflower Soap

This light, fresh soap has a clean floral scent. The sunflower and castor oils used in this soap condition and smooth the skin. With its light fragrance and sunny yellow color, sunflower soap is the perfect recipe to pamper your skin in the summertime.

Ingredients

- 2 ounces (57g) castor oil
- 12 ounces (341g) coconut oil
- 24 ounces (682g) olive oil
- 8 ounces (227g) sunflower oil
- 8 ounces (227g) palm kernel oil
- 7.6 ounces (216g) lye
- 20 ounces (568g) distilled water
- ⅛ teaspoon (0.6ml) FD&C yellow #5
- 2.5 ounces (74ml) sunflower fragrance oil

design TIP

• • • • •

For added texture and color, add calendula petals, which remain yellow throughout the soapmaking process. Add them when you add the fragrance oil.

1. Place the measuring cup on the scale and push the tare button to zero the scale. Add 20 ounces (568g) of distilled water.

2. In a glass or stainless steel measuring cup, measure 7.6 ounces (216g) of lye. Again, remember to tare the scale to zero.

3. In a well-ventilated area, add the lye into the distilled water while stirring with a long-handled plastic spoon.

4. Once all of the lye has dissolved in the water, neutralize the lye residue on the long-handled plastic spoon and glass measuring cup with your soapy vinegar mixture. Set the lye water aside, safely out of the way.

5. Place your enamel or stainless steel pot on the scale and push the tare button to zero the scale. Measure out the solid oils and heat them on low heat on the stove or in a slow cooker.

6. Measure the liquid oils in a glass measuring cup.

7. Once the solid oils have melted, combine with the liquid oils in either a slow cooker, large roaster or double boiler. Stir the oils for uniformity.

8. Slowly and carefully, add the lye water to the oils. Stick blend thoroughly. Neutralize the measuring cup with the soapy vinegar mixture.

9. At this point add the yellow #5 colorant.

10. Continue to stick blend until the soap mixture reaches trace.

11. Cook the soap.

12. Once the soap has fully saponified, add the sunflower fragrance oil and any natural additives if you so choose.

13. Next, add the soap mixture to the mold of your choice. Be sure to either line the mold with a plastic trash bag or spray the mold with olive oil. Allow the soap to sit for 4–6 hours and enjoy!

YIELDS 54 OUNCES (1.5KG) OF SOAP

Kitchen Soap

When you are cooking with something very pungent, this soap will remove the smell from your hands. It is a lifesaver when it comes to removing the smell of onions, garlic and fish. The secret to this de-scenting soap is the coffee required in the recipe. Without any colorants, this soap turns dark brown in color. You can lighten it to a beige or tan with oil dispersible titanium dioxide.

Ingredients

- 8 ounces (227g) avocado oil
- 2 ounces (58g) castor oil
- 10 ounces (284g) coconut oil
- 24 ounces (682g) olive oil
- 8 ounces (227g) palm kernel oil
- 2 ounces (57g) wheat germ oil
- 20 ounces (568g) cold strong coffee (brewed with distilled water)
- 7.5 ounces (213g) lye
- 1 ounce (28g) cinnamon fragrance oil
- 1½ tablespoon (23ml) oil dispersible titanium dioxide

1. Using distilled water, brew approximately 20 ounces (568g) of strong coffee. After it has brewed, put it in the refrigerator until cooled.

2. Measure out 7.5 ounces (213g) of lye in a measuring cup, using your digital scale.

3. In a well-ventilated area, add the lye into the cold, strong coffee while stirring with a long-handled plastic spoon.

4. Using your enamel pot, measure out the coconut and palm kernel oils. Remember to tare the scale to get accurate measurements. Heat the solid oils on a low heat using either a slow cooker or the stovetop.

5. While the solid oils are melting, measure the liquid oils in a large measuring cup. Set aside.

6. Neutralize the long-handled plastic spoon and glass measuring cup with your soapy vinegar mixture. Set the lye and coffee mixture aside, safely out of the way.

7. Once the solid oils have melted, combine them with the liquid oils in either the slow cooker, large roaster or double boiler. Stir the oils for uniform consistency.

8. Slowly add the lye and coffee mixture to the oils. Stick blend thoroughly.

9. Add the oil dispersible titanium dioxide and blend thoroughly to trace.

10. While the soap saponifies and cooks, neutralize the measuring cups and stick blender blades in the soapy vinegar mixture.

11. Once the soap has fully saponified, add the cinnamon fragrance oil. Put the soap mixture into the mold of your choice. Be sure to line the mold with either a plastic trash bag, freezer paper or spray the plastic mold with olive oil. Once the soap has hardened, remove from the molds and enjoy!

YIELDS 54 OUNCES (1.5KG) OF SOAP

design TIP

Often, hunters will use the unscented version of this recipe to remove human scent. If you decide to make this as a hunter's soap, do not add any fragrance oils.

Perfect for sensitive skin, castile soap is one of the simplest and oldest recipes you can make. Castile soap originated in Castile, Spain and is 100% olive oil. There is an American castile soap, but this version can contain as little as 51% olive oil. Compare a variety of olive oil grades and create true castile soap, as it was originally made in Spain centuries ago.

Ingredients

- 54 ounces (1.5kg) olive oil
- 16 ounces (454g) distilled water
- 7 ounces (199g) lye
- 1 ounce (28g) of pearberry fragrance oil (optional)

1. In a measuring cup, carefully measure 16 ounces (454g) of distilled water. Then, in a glass or stainless steel measuring cup, measure 7 ounces (199g) of lye. Remember to tare the scale to get accurate measurements.

2. In a well-ventilated area, add the lye into the distilled water while stirring with a long-handled spoon.

3. Measure the olive oil in a glass measuring cup. Pour the oil into either a slow cooker, large roaster or double boiler.

4. Once all of the lye has dissolved in the distilled water, neutralize the lye residue on the long-handled plastic spoon and glass measuring cup with your soapy vinegar mixture.

5. Slowly and carefully add the lye water to the olive oil. Stick blend thoroughly. Neutralize the measuring cup in the soapy vinegar mixture.

6. Continue to stick blend until the soap mixture reaches trace.

7. Cook the soap through saponification.

8. Stir to cool down the soap. Add the pearberry fragrance oil. If you have very sensitive skin, you may not want to add any fragrance at all. However, you may want to add a mild scent like pearberry, that slightly masks the olive oil's scent.

9. Add the soap mixture to the mold of your choice. Be sure to either line the mold with a plastic trash bag or spray the mold with olive oil.

10. Allow the soap to harden for 4–6 hours. When the soap is ready, remove it from the mold and enjoy.

YIELDS 54 OUNCES (1.5KG) OF SOAP

design TIP

When making a 100% olive oil recipe, you may find that the soap initially feels slimy, producing very little bubbles. Allow this soap to dry out for a few weeks up to three months. It will turn very white and lather well.

Energizing Citrus Soap

Wake up in the morning with this invigorating bar of soap! This recipe is a great way to start your day. The citrus fragrance stimulates your senses while the oils used in this recipe will pamper your skin. The castor, sunflower, cocoa butter and shea butter are wonderful conditioners, creating a bar of soap with an excellent combination of oils to help soften your skin.

Ingredients

- 8 ounces (227g) sunflower oil
- 2 ounces (57g) castor oil
- 4 ounces (114g) cocoa butter
- 12 ounces (341g) coconut oil
- 24 ounces (681g) olive oil
- 4 ounces (227g) shea butter
- 20 ounces (567g) distilled water
- 7.4 ounces (210g) lye
- 1 ounce (28g) mandarin orange fragrance oil
- 1 teaspoon (5ml) orange oxide

design TIP

- - - - -

Add poppy seeds to this recipe to give this soap exfoliating properties. Use approximately ¼ cup (60ml) for this recipe. Add the poppy seeds after you add the fragrance oils.

1. Carefully measure out 20 ounces (568g) of distilled water. Place the measuring cup on the scale and push the tare button.

2. In a glass or stainless steel measuring cup, measure 7.4 ounces (210g) of lye.

3. In a well-ventilated area, add the lye into the distilled water while stirring with a long-handled plastic spoon.

4. Once all of the lye has dissolved in the water, neutralize the lye residue on the long-handled plastic spoon and glass measuring cup with your soapy vinegar mixture. Set the lye water aside, out of the way and out of reach of children.

5. Place your enamel pot on the scale and tare to zero. Measure out the solid oils and butters and heat them on a low heat on the stove or in a slow cooker.

6. Measure the liquid oils in a glass measuring cup. Once the solid oils have melted, combine them with the liquid oils in either the slow cooker, large roaster or double boiler. Stir the oils for uniformity.

7. Slowly and carefully, add the lye water to the oils. Stick blend thoroughly. Neutralize the measuring cup with the soapy vinegar mixture.

8. At this point add the orange oxide colorant to the soap mixture.

9. Continue to stick blend until the soap mixture reaches trace.

10. Cook the soap.

11. Once the soap has fully saponified, allow it to cool slightly before adding the mandarin orange fragrance oil.

12. Add the soap mixture to the mold of your choice. Be sure to either line the mold with a plastic trash bag or spray the mold with olive oil.

13. Allow the soap to sit for 4–6 hours. When the soap has hardened, carefully remove from the molds and enjoy!

YIELDS 54 OUNCES (1.5KG) OF SOAP

The scent of lavender has a calming, soothing effect, which can help you relax after a busy day. Lavender essential oil is usually combined with other essential oils like rosemary and patchouli, but it can be used alone as well. It is pleasant and strong enough to hold the scent through the soapmaking process. Be sure to sample a variety lavender essential oils before choosing one in your recipe.

Ingredients

- 8 ounces (227g) almond oil
- 2 ounces (57g) castor oil
- 8 ounces (227g) coconut oil
- 36 ounces (1kg) olive oil
- 16 ounces (454g) distilled water
- 7.3 ounces (207g) lye
- ⅛ teaspoon (0.6ml) FD&C #1
- 1.5 ounces (43g) lavender essential oil
- 0.5 ounce (14g) patchouli essential oil
- 0.5 ounce (14g) rosemary essential oil

design
TIP
• • • • •

As a variation, keep this bar of soap white and add dried lavender buds for texture when you add the fragrance.

1. Carefully measure out the distilled water. Place the measuring cup on the scale and push the tare button. Add 16 ounces (454g) of distilled water.

2. In a glass or stainless steel measuring cup, measure 7.3 ounces (207g) of lye.

3. In a well-ventilated area, add the lye into the water while stirring with a long-handled plastic spoon.

4. Once all of the lye has dissolved in the water, neutralize the long-handled spoon and glass measuring cup with your soapy vinegar mixture. Set the lye water aside, out of the way and out of reach of children.

5. Place your enamel pot on the scale and tare to zero. Measure out the coconut oil on low heat on the stove or in the slow cooker.

6. Once the coconut oil has melted, combine it with the liquid oils in either the slow cooker, large roaster or double boiler. Stir the oils for uniformity.

7. Slowly and carefully, add the lye water to the oils. Stick blend thoroughly until the soap mixture reaches trace.

8. Neutralize the measuring cup in the soapy vinegar mixture.

9. Cook the soap.

10. Once the soap has fully saponified, add the colorants. Start with ¹⁄₁₆ teaspoon (0.3ml) of FD&C #1. It will mix with the soap mixture at trace and produce a red raspberry color. Then add ¹⁄₁₆ teaspoon (0.3ml) more of the FD&C #1 to ½ ounce (15ml) of water. This will turn a deep blue color. Add the deep blue after the cook to produce lavender.

11. Add the essential oils. Be sure to allow the soap to cool slightly first. Then add the soap mixture to the mold of your choice. Line the mold with either a plastic trash bag or spray the mold with olive oil.

12. Once the soap has hardened, carefully remove from the mold and enjoy!

MAKES 54 OUNCES (1.5KG) OF SOAP

Green Tea Soap

Renew your skin with vitamin C and E from the green tea used in this simple vegetable soap recipe. Green tea provides natural antioxidant benefits to the body and can help repair skin damage caused by the environment. At the same time, this soap will leave your skin feeling fresh and clean.

Ingredients

- 8 ounces (227g) almond oil
- 8 ounces (227g) avocado oil
- 12 ounces (341g) coconut oil
- 24 ounces (682g) olive oil
- 16 ounces (454g) cold green tea (brewed with distilled water)
- 7.2 ounces (204g) lye
- 1 teaspoon (5ml) green oxide
- 2.5 ounces (71g) green tea fragrance oil

1. With distilled water, brew approximately 16 ounces (454g) of green tea. After it has brewed, put it in the refrigerator until cooled.

2. In a glass or stainless steel measuring cup, measure 7.2 ounces (204g) of lye. Again, tare the scale before you take a measurement.

3. In a well-ventilated area, add the lye into the green tea while stirring with a long-handled plastic spoon.

4. Once all of the lye has dissolved, neutralize the spoon and glass measuring cup with your soapy vinegar mixture.

5. Measure the coconut oil in your enamel pot. Be sure to always tare the scale to get an accurate measurement. Heat the solid oils on low heat while you prepare the other ingredients.

6. Slowly and carefully, add the lye and green tea mixture to the oils. Stick blend thoroughly. Again neutralize the measuring cup with the soapy vinegar mixture.

7. At this point add the green oxide. Continue to stick blend until the soap mixture reaches trace.

8. Cook the soap. After the soap has saponified, allow the mixture to cool slightly. Then add the green tea fragrance oil.

9. Add the soap mixture to the mold of your choice. Be sure to line the mold with a plastic trash bag or spray it with olive oil.

10. Allow the soap to sit and dry out for 4–6 hours. When the soap has hardened, carefully remove from the molds and enjoy your luxury bar!

MAKES 52 OUNCES (1.5KG) OF SOAP

design TIP

For added texture and visual interest, add green tea leaves from the tea bags you used in step 1. Coat them in a light oil and add them to the recipe with the fragrance.

A fragrant blend of fresh peaches with a light floral scent produces a soap with a subtle spring-time fragrance. It is difficult to find a pure peach fragrance that works well in soap, however this recipe has a fruity scent along with a floral bouquet. The result is a balanced scent that is not too overpowering. The fragrance is added to economical oils for a truly wonderful bar of soap.

Ingredients

• 12 ounces (341g) canola oil

• 2 ounces (57g) castor oil

• 12 ounces (341g) coconut oil

• 24 ounces (682g) olive oil

• 6 ounces (170g) palm oil

• 20 ounces (568g) distilled water

• 7.8 ounces (222g) lye

• ⅛ teaspoon (.6ml) FD&C orange #5

• 2.5 ounces (71g) Georgia peach fragrance oil

design TIP

. . . . .

Palm oil naturally gives a yellow to orange tint to the soap, so remember to take this into consideration when using color additives.

1. Place a measuring cup on the scale and tare to zero. Add 20 ounces (568g) of distilled water.

2. In a glass or stainless steel measuring cup, measure 7.8 ounces (222g) of lye.

3. In a well-ventilated area, add the lye into the distilled water while stirring with a long-handled spoon.

4. Once all of the lye has dissolved in the water, neutralize the spoon and glass measuring cup with your soapy vinegar mixture. Set the lye water aside, out of the way and out of reach of children.

5. Place your enamel pot on the scale and push the tare button. Measure out the coconut and palm oils and heat them on low heat on the stove or in the slow cooker.

6. Measure the liquid oils in a glass measuring cup. Set aside.

7. Once the solid oils have melted, combine them with the liquid oils in either the slow cooker, large roaster or double boiler. Stir the oils for uniformity.

8. Slowly and carefully, add the lye water to the oils. Stick blend thoroughly.

9. At this point add the FD&C orange #5.

10. Continue to stick blend until the soap mixture reaches trace.

11. Cook the soap.

12. Once the soap has fully saponified, add the Georgia peach fragrance oil. Then add the soap mixture to the mold of your choice. Line the mold with a plastic trash bag or spray it with olive oil.

13. When the soap has hardened, carefully remove from the molds and enjoy your handcrafted soap.

MAKES 56 OUNCES (1.6KG) OF SOAP

The invigorating seashore scent of this soap will make you feel like you are on vacation every time you use it. This recipe is fun because you can find many molds with an ocean theme, such as sea horses, sailboats, seashells and fish. The base oils used in this recipe are all economical, making this a great recipe for new soapmakers to try. This fresh and outdoorsy-scented soap, is popular with both men and women.

Ingredients

- 24 ounces (682g) canola oil
- 2 ounces (57g) castor oil
- 6 ounces (170g) coconut oil
- 24 ounces (682g) olive oil
- 16 ounces (454g) distilled water
- 7.5 ounces (213g) lye
- 2.5 ounces (71g) seashore fragrance oil
- 1 teaspoon (5ml) FD&C #3 green
- ⅛ teaspoon (.6ml) black oxide

design TIP

The seashore fragrance in this soap is very versatile. Consider blending floral or fruity scents with it to come up with a unique, aromatic recipe of your own.

1 Carefully measure out 16 ounces of distilled water on your digital scale. Remember to tare the scale to ensure accurate measurements.

2 In a glass or stainless steel measuring cup, measure 7.5 ounces (213g) of lye. Again, tare the scale before you take a measurement.

3 In a well-ventilated area, add the lye into the distilled water while stirring with a long-handled plastic spoon.

4 Once all of the lye has dissolved, neutralize the spoon and measuring cup with soapy vinegar mixture.

5 Place your enamel pot on the scale and push the tare button. Measure out the solid oils and heat them on a low heat on the stove or in the slow cooker. While the solid oils are melting, carefully measure out the liquid oils.

6 Once the solid oils have melted, combine them with the liquid oils in either the slow cooker, large roaster or double boiler. Stir the oils for uniformity.

7 Slowly and carefully, add the lye water to the oils. Stick blend thoroughly.

8 At this point add the FD&C #3 color additive.

9 Continue to stick blend until the soap mixture reaches trace.

10 Cook the soap through saponification.

11 Once the soap has fully saponified, add the seashore fragrance oil. Then add the soap mixture to the molds of your choice. Be sure to line the mold with either a plastic trash bag or spray it with olive oil.

12 Allow the soap to sit for 4–6 hours. When the soap has hardened, carefully remove it from the mold and enjoy your luxury bar!

YIELDS 56 OUNCES (1.6KG) OF SOAP

Stir your senses with this wonderfully fragrant recipe, made with rose petals fragrance oil. The bouquet is subtle and not too overpowering. Do not use rose water because the fragrance will not hold up through saponification. A good quality synthetic oil produces a lovely soap with a timeless and true rose fragrance.

Ingredients

- 16 ounces (454g) canola oil
- 2 ounces (57g) castor oil
- 8 ounces (227g) coconut oil
- 30 ounces (850g) olive oil
- 16 ounces (454g) distilled water
- 7.5 ounces (213g) lye
- 1.5 ounces (43g) rose petals fragrance oil
- 1 teaspoon (5ml) FD&C #30 lake

1. Place a measuring cup on the digital scale and press the tare button. Carefully measure out 16 ounces (454g) of distilled water.

2. In a glass or stainless steel measuring cup, measure 7.5 ounces (213g) of lye. Be sure to tare the scale.

3. In a well-ventilated area, add the lye into the water while stirring with a long-handled spoon.

4. Once all of the lye has dissolved in the water, neutralize the lye residue on the spoon and measuring cup with your soapy vinegar mixture.

5. Place your enamel pot on the scale and tare to zero. Measure out the solid oils and melt them on a low heat.

6. Once the solid oils have melted, combine them with the liquid oils in either the slow cooker, large roaster or double boiler. Stir the oils for uniformity.

7. Slowly and carefully, add the lye water to the oils.

8. Add the FD&C #30 color additive to the soap mixture. Continue to stick blend until the soap mixture reaches trace.

9. Cook the soap. Once the soap has fully saponified, add the rose petals fragrance oil.

10. Place the soap mixture into the mold of your choice. Be sure to either line the mold with a plastic trash bag or spray it with olive oil. Allow the soap to sit for 4–6 hours.

11. When the soap has hardened, carefully remove from the mold and enjoy your handcrafted romantic rose soap!

YIELDS 56 OUNCES (1.6KG) OF SOAP

design TIP

Roses are classic, and this recipe would make a wonderful gift for the special women in your life. Be creative by using heart-shaped or floral molds.

This luxurious, creamy bar of soap smells and feels decadent! Use the non-discoloring fragrance oil as opposed to the regular vanilla fragrance oil to produce a cream-colored bar of soap, as opposed to a dark brown. Indulge your senses and your skin with this wonderful bar of soap!

Ingredients

- 12 ounces (341g) avocado oil
- 2 ounces (57g) castor oil
- 4 ounces (114g) cocoa butter
- 8 ounces (227g) coconut oil
- 24 ounces (682g) olive oil
- 4 ounces (114g) shea butter
- 20 ounces (568g) of distilled water
- 7.1 ounces (202g) lye
- 2.5 ounces (71g) non-discoloring vanilla fragrance oil

design TIP
• • • • •

Non-discoloring vanilla fragrance oil blends well with bitter or pungent fragrance oils, because it sweetens and softens the overall fragrance.

1. Carefully measure out 20 ounces (568g) of distilled water on your digital scale. Remember to tare the scale to ensure accurate measurements.

2. In a glass or stainless steel measuring cup, measure 7.1 ounces (202g) of lye. Measure the liquid oils in a glass measuring cup. Set aside.

3. In a well-ventilated area, add the lye into the distilled water while stirring with a long-handled plastic spoon.

4. Once all of the lye has dissolved, neutralize the lye residue on the long-handled spoon and glass measuring cup with your soapy vinegar mixture. Set the lye water aside, out of the way and out of the reach of children.

5. Place your enamel pot on the scale and push the tare button. Measure out the cocoa butter, shea butter and coconut oil and heat them on low heat on the stove or in the slow cooker.

6. Once the solid oils have melted, combine with the liquid oils in either the slow cooker, large roaster or double boiler. Stir the oils for uniformity.

7. Slowly and carefully, add the lye water to the oils.

8. Continue to stick blend until the soap mixture reaches trace.

9. Cook the soap.

10. Once the soap has fully saponified, add the non-discoloring vanilla fragrance oil. Then, add the soap mixture to the mold of your choice. Line the mold with a plastic trash bag or spray it with olive oil.

11. Allow the soap to sit for 4–6 hours. When the soap has hardened, carefully remove from the mold and enjoy!

MAKES 54 OUNCES (1.5KG) OF SOAP

Man's best friend can use a little pampering too. This recipe will give your dog a noticeably healthier, shinier coat. Not only will the coat feel softer and stronger, the soap will help keep little pests like fleas and ticks away, too! He really will be your best friend after a doggie bath with this bar.

84

Ingredients

- 2 ounces (57g) castor oil
- 7 ounces (199g) coconut oil
- 10 ounces (284g) olive oil
- 5 ounces (142g) palm kernel oil
- 8 ounces (227g) safflower oil
- 10 ounces (284g) distilled water
- 4.5 ounces (128g) lye
- 0.7 ounce (20g) lavender essential oil
- 0.1 ounce (3g) tea tree essential oil
- 0.2 ounce (6g) eucalyptus essential oil
- 0.5 ounce (14g) fir needle essential oil
- 0.1 ounce (3g) patchouli essential oil

1. Place your measuring cup on the scale and tare to zero. Carefully measure out 10 ounces (284g) of distilled water.

2. Carefully measure out 4.5 ounces (128g) of lye in a glass or stainless steel measuring cup.

3. In a well-ventilated area, add the lye into the distilled water while stirring with a long-handled plastic spoon.

4. Once all of the lye has dissolved in the water, neutralize the lye residue on the long-handled plastic spoon and glass measuring cup with your soapy vinegar mixture. Set the lye water aside, out of the way and out of the reach of children.

5. Measure out the coconut and palm kernel oils and heat them on a low heat on the stove or in a slow cooker.

6. Once the solid oils have melted, combine them with the liquid oils in either the slow cooker, large roaster or double boiler. Stir the oils for uniformity.

7. Slowly and carefully, add the lye water to the oils. Stick blend thoroughly.

8. Continue to stick blend until the soap mixture reaches trace.

9. Cook the soap.

10. Once the soap has fully saponified, add the essential oils.

11. Place the soap into a mold. Line the mold with a plastic trash bag or spray with olive oil. Allow the soap to sit for 4–6 hours. When the soap has hardened, carefully remove from the mold and share it with your favorite dog!

MAKES 32 OUNCES (909G) OF SOAP

design
TIP

• • • •

Talk to your veterinarian before making any variations or substitutions in this recipe. Do not use this soap on any other animal without your veterinarian's approval.

* Woof is a registered trademark of Nardi's Suds, Issaquah, Washington.

The fresh, wildberry scent added to this cocoa butter soap recipe will produce a wonderfully fragrant, highly moisturizing bar of soap. When you use nonrefined cocoa butter, there is a strong, natural chocolate scent. The chocolate and wildberry complement each other to produce an exquisite, aromatic bar of soap.

Ingredients

- 2 ounces (57g) castor oil
- 4 ounces (114g) cocoa butter
- 12 ounces (341g) coconut oil
- 12 ounces (341g) grapeseed oil
- 24 ounces (682g) olive oil
- 16 ounces (454g) distilled water
- 7.4 ounces (210g) lye
- 2.5 ounces (71g) wildberry fragrance oil
- 1 teaspoon (5ml) FD&C red #33
- 1/8 teaspoon (.6ml) black oxide

design TIP

When creating your own Wildberry soap, you do not need to find a specific wildberry fragrance oil, because wildberry is a general description. Sample various berry fragrance oils and come up with your own personal favorite.

1. Place your measuring cup on the scale and tare to zero. Carefully measure out 16 ounces (454g) of distilled water.

2. In a glass or stainless steel measuring cup, measure 7.4 ounces (210g) of lye.

3. In a well-ventilated area, add the lye into the distilled water while stirring with a long-handled plastic spoon.

4. Once all of the lye has dissolved in the water, neutralize the lye residue on the long-handled plastic spoon and glass measuring cup with your soapy vinegar mixture. Set the lye water aside, out of the way and out of the reach of children.

5. Measure out the coconut oil and cocoa butter and heat them on low heat on the stove or in a slow cooker.

6. Once the solid oils have melted, combine them with the liquid oils in either the slow cooker, large roaster or double boiler. Stir the oils for uniformity.

7. Slowly and carefully, add the lye water to the oils. Stick blend thoroughly.

8. At this point, add the FD&C red #33 and the black oxide color additive.

9. Continue to stick blend until the soap mixture reaches trace.

10. Cook the soap through saponification.

11. Once the soap has fully saponified, add the essential oils.

12. Place the soap into a mold. Line the mold with a plastic trash bag or spray with olive oil. Allow the soap to sit for 4–6 hours. Once the soap has hardened, remove from the mold and enjoy.

MAKES 54 OUNCES (1.5KG) OF SOAP

Mint Medley Soap

The refreshing scents of peppermint, eucalyptus and rosemary essential oils featured in this recipe make a stimulating bar of soap. The combination not only adds complexity to the fragrance, but also dilutes the peppermint, which can be irritating to your skin. At the same time the shea butter helps to soothe and condition the skin.

Ingredients

- 8 ounces (227g) avocado oil
- 2 ounces (57g) castor oil
- 10 ounces (284g) coconut oil
- 24 ounces (682g) olive oil
- 8 ounces (227g) palm kernel oil
- 6 ounces (170g) shea butter
- 22 ounces (625g) distilled water
- 7.8 ounces (222g) lye
- 0.5 ounce (14g) eucalyptus essential oil
- 0.5 ounce (14g) peppermint essential oil
- 0.5 ounce (14g) rosemary essential oil
- ¼ teaspoon (1ml) hydrated chromium oxide

design TIP

• • • • •

Try other fragrance combinations in this recipe like lavender or orange scents. This recipe is very versatile because of the variety of fragrances you can blend.

1. Place your measuring cup on the scale and tare to zero. Carefully measure out 22 ounces (625g) of distilled water.

2. Measure 7.8 ounces (222g) of lye in a glass or stainless steel measuring cup.

3. In a well-ventilated area, add the lye into the distilled water while stirring with a long-handled plastic spoon.

4. Once all of the lye has dissolved in the water, neutralize the lye residue on the long-handled plastic spoon and glass measuring cup with your soapy vinegar mixture. Set the lye water aside, out of the way and out of the reach of children.

5. Measure out the coconut oil, palm kernel oil, and shea butter, and heat them on a low heat on the stove or in a slow cooker until they have melted.

6. Once the solid oils have melted, combine them with the liquid oils in either the slow cooker, large roaster or double boiler. Stir the oils for uniformity.

7. Slowly and carefully, add the lye water to the oils. Stick blend thoroughly.

8. Add the hydrated chromium oxide to the mixture.

9. Continue to stick blend until the soap mixture reaches trace.

10. Cook the soap.

11. Once the soap has fully saponified, add the eucalyptus, peppermint and rosemary essential oils.

12. Line the mold with a plastic trash bag or spray with olive oil. Add the soap mixture to the mold. Allow the soap to sit for 4–6 hours. The soap is ready to use after it has hardened. Enjoy!

MAKES 58 OUNCES (1.6KG) OF SOAP

Replenishing Soap

This soap will heal and soothe dry and rough skin, as well as treat eczema and many other skin conditions. Shea butter, avocado oil and emu oil all have skin restoring properties that nourish and rejuvenate, while the lavender, rosemary and tea tree essential oils all have healing properties.

Ingredients

- 4 ounces (114g) avocado oil
- 2 ounces (57g) castor oil
- 12 ounces (341g) coconut oil
- 8 ounces (227g) emu oil
- 24 ounces (682g) olive oil
- 4 ounces (114g) shea butter
- 2 ounces (57g) wheat germ oil
- 16 ounces (454g) distilled water
- 7.6 ounces (216g) lye
- 1.5 ounces (43g) lavender essential oil
- 0.5 ounce (14g) rosemary essential oil
- 0.5 ounce (14g) tea tree essential oil

1. Place your measuring cup on the scale and tare to zero. Carefully measure out 16 ounces (454g) of distilled water.

2. Carefully measure out 7.6 ounces (216g) of lye in a glass or stainless steel measuring cup.

3. In a well-ventilated area, add the lye into the distilled water while stirring with a long-handled plastic spoon.

4. Once all of the lye has dissolved in the water, neutralize the lye residue on the long-handled plastic spoon and glass measuring cup with your soapy vinegar mixture. Set the lye water aside, out of the way and out of the reach of children.

5. Place your enamel pot on the scale and tare to zero. Measure out the coconut oil and shea butter and heat them on a low heat on the stove or in a slow cooker.

6. Once the solid oils have melted, combine them with the liquid oils in either the slow cooker, large roaster or double boiler. Stir the oils for uniformity.

7. Slowly and carefully, add the lye water to the oils. Stick blend thoroughly.

8. Continue to stick blend until the soap mixture reaches trace.

9. Cook the soap.

10. Once the soap has fully saponified, add the lavender, rosemary and tea tree essential oils.

11. Place the soap into a mold. Line the mold with a plastic trash bag or spray with olive oil. Allow the soap to sit for 4–6 hours. Then, carefully remove from the mold and enjoy!

MAKES 56 OUNCES (1.6KG) OF SOAP

design TIP

* * * *

Depending on your preference, you may want to use a little less or a little more of the essential oils. Adjust the amount of essential oils, but maintain the ratio 3 parts lavender, to 1 part rosemary, to 1 part tea tree oil.

Chamomile Soap

The Chamomile flower is known for its soothing and calming effect. The essential oil is costly, so try a quality fragrance oil. With the bergamot citrus blend, it enhances the chamomile scent. For a full effect, relax in a bathtub and sip herbal tea and enjoy this bar of soap.

Ingredients

- 2 ounces (57g) castor oil
- 8 ounces (227g) almond oil
- 8 ounces (227g) apricot kernel oil
- 16 ounces (454g) coconut oil
- 24 ounces (682g) olive oil
- 22 ounces (625g) cold chamomile tea (brewed with distilled water)
- 8.1 ounces (230g) lye
- 1 teaspoon (5ml) yellow oxide
- ¼–½ cup (59ml–118ml) dried chamomile
- 2.5 ounces (71g) chamomile bergamot fragrance oil

design
TIP
• • • •

Add calendula petals instead of tea leaves. Unlike the chamomile, calendula petals maintain their yellow color throughout the soapmaking process.

1. Carefully measure 22 ounces (625g) of distilled water in a measuring cup on your digital scale. With this water, brew strong chamomile tea with three tea bags. Place it in the refrigerator until it is cool.

2. Carefully measure out 8.1 ounces (230g) of lye in a glass or stainless steel measuring cup. Remember to tare the scale to get an accurate reading.

3. In a well-ventilated area, add the lye into the distilled water while stirring with a long-handled plastic spoon.

4. Once all of the lye has dissolved in the water, neutralize the lye residue on the long-handled plastic spoon and glass measuring cup with your soapy vinegar mixture. Set the lye water aside, out of the way and out of the reach of children.

5. Place your enamel or stainless steel pot on your scale and measure out the coconut oil. Heat it on low until melted.

6. Once the solid oil has melted, combine it with the liquid oils in either the slow cooker, large roaster or double boiler. Stir the oils for uniformity.

7. Slowly and carefully, add the lye water to the oils. Stick blend thoroughly.

8. Add 1 teaspoon (5ml) of yellow oxide and continue to stick blend until the mixture reaches trace.

9. Cook the soap.

10. Once the soap has fully saponified, add the chamomile bergamot fragrance oil and the dried chamomile.

11. Add the soap to the mold of your choice. Line the mold with a plastic trash bag or spray it with an olive oil spray. Allow the soap to harden, and carefully remove from the mold and enjoy your soothing chamomile soap!

MAKES 58 OUNCES (1.6KG) OF SOAP

Oatmeal, Milk & Honey Soap

Pamper your skin through the winter months with this conditioning bar of soap. Oatmeal is a natural exfoliant and removes dry, flaky skin. The goat milk makes the soap creamy and nourishes the skin. And the honey, which is a natural humectant, draws moisture to the skin. For additional tips on making milk soaps, see pages 46–47.

Ingredients

- 8 ounces (227g) canola oil
- 2 ounces (57g) castor oil
- 4 ounces (114g) cocoa butter
- 14 ounces (398g) coconut oil
- 24 ounces (682g) olive oil
- 8 ounces (227g) safflower oil
- 22 ounces (625g) distilled water
- 8.2 ounces (233g) lye
- 2.5 ounces (71g) brown sugar fragrance oil
- 0.5 ounce (14g) honey
- 2 tablespoons (30ml) powdered goat milk
- 2 ounces (57g) coarsely ground oats

1. Carefully measure out the distilled water. Take two plastic measuring cups and fill each of them with 2.75 ounces (78g) of distilled water. The remaining 16.5 ounces (469g) of distilled water will be used to combine with the lye. Remember to tare the scale to ensure accurate measurements.

2. Measure out 2 tablespoons (30ml) of powdered goat milk. Whisk the goat milk in one of the 2.75 ounces (78g) of water. Stir in honey in the other 2.75 ounces (78g) of water. Place both of these plastic cups in the freezer.

3. Place a glass measuring cup on your scale and measure 8.2 ounces (233g) of lye. In a well-ventilated area, add the lye into the 16.5 ounces (469g) of distilled water while stirring with a long-handled plastic spoon.

4. Once all of the lye has dissolved in the water, neutralize the long-handled plastic spoon and measuring cup with your soapy vinegar mixture.

5. Measure out the coconut and palm kernel oils and heat them on a low heat on the stove or in a slow cooker.

6. Once the solid oils have melted, combine them with the liquid oils in either the slow cooker, large roaster or double boiler. Stir the oils for uniformity.

7. Slowly and carefully, add the lye water to the oils. Stick blend thoroughly until the mixture reaches trace.

8. Cook the soap.

9. Once the soap has fully saponified, add the brown sugar fragrance oil and the coarsely ground oats.

10. Add the icy honey water and icy goat milk to the soap mixture.

11. Line the mold with a plastic trash bag or spray with olive oil and add the soap mixture. Once the soap has hardened, carefully remove from the mold and enjoy your handcrafted soap!

design
TIP

When storing this soap in the shower, it is best to keep it in a soap dish that does not collect water. Otherwise, the soap will become soggy very quickly, especially with the oats.

MAKES 60 OUNCES (1.7KG) OF SOAP

The following recipes give the base oils, lye and water. You may add the color additives, fragrances and natural additives of your choice, as explained on pages 15–19. This is a great way to experiment with your favorite fragrances and color additives. While all of the recipes thus far in this book have been made with plant-based oils, in this section I have also included a few recipes using animal fats, lard and tallow. Animal fats help harden soap, but do not provide much conditioning on their own, with the exception of emu oil. All-vegetable oils recipes are often preferred by soapmakers because they are generally more conditioning and noncomedogenic (won't clog pores). However, try both plant oils and animal fats in your recipe to see which you prefer. Pick your favorites and have fun experimenting!

Vegetable Oil Soaps

⊛ Boone's Lather Goat Milk Soap

Goat milk makes a very creamy, moisturizing, 100% milk soap. This original recipe produces a white bar of soap. Try adding Yuzu, a Japanese fragrance, to give it a wonderfully fresh scent. Or, use brown sugar fragrance oil, which smells sweet, giving it a honey scent.

    8 ounces (227g) almond oil
    2 ounces (57g) castor oil
    12 ounces (341g) coconut oil
    24 ounces (682g) olive oil
    8 ounces (227g) palm kernel oil
    4 ounces (114g) emu oil
    22 ounces (625g) distilled water
    8.2 ounces (233g) lye
    12 tablespoons (177ml) powdered goat milk

YIELDS 58 OUNCES (1.6KG) OF SOAP

⊛ Boone's Lather Shampoo & Body Bar

For a clean, refreshing fragrance in your shampoo bar, use a mixture of lavender, rosemary, sweet orange, bitter orange and dark patchouli. Add a dash of peppermint for a slight zing. Play with the fragrances you like best.

    16 ounces (454g) avocado oil
    8 ounces (227g) castor oil
    24 ounces (682g) coconut oil
    48 ounces (1.4kg) olive oil
    16 ounces (454g) palm kernel oil
    16 ounces (454g) emu oil
    44 ounces (1.2kg) distilled water
    17.7 ounces (503g) lye

YIELDS 128 OUNCES (3.6KG) OF SOAP

American Castile Soap

Unlike Spanish castile soap, American castile uses more oils than just olive oil. This recipe still provides the gentle cleansing you would expect from Spanish castile soap. Try scenting this soap with florals like violet or fresh scents like pearberry.

8 ounces (227g) almond oil
2 ounces (57g) castor oil
8 ounces (227g) coconut oil
36 ounces (1kg) olive oil
16 ounces (454g) distilled water
7.3 ounces (207g) lye

YIELDS 54 OUNCES (1.5KG) OF SOAP

Simply Vegetable Soap

Because avocado and olive oils may naturally give off a green color, try adding cooling scents like green tea, forest, seashore or other minty or herbal scents to this recipe.

8 ounces (227g) almond oil
8 ounces (227g) avocado oil
12 ounces (341g) coconut oil
24 ounces (682g) olive oil
8 ounces (227g) palm kernel oil
4 ounces (114g) emu oil
16 ounces (454g) distilled water
7.2 ounces (204g) lye

YIELDS 52 OUNCES (1.5KG) OF SOAP

Palmola Soap

Since palm oil can cause your soap to take on a yellow to orange tint, this would be a perfect recipe for fragrance oils like amber, bay rum or peach.

12 ounces (340g) canola oil
2 ounces (57g) castor oil
12 ounces (340g) coconut oil
24 ounces (680g) olive oil
6 ounces (170g) palm oil
20 ounces (567g) distilled water
7.8 ounces (221g) lye

YIELDS 56 OUNCES (1.6KG) OF SOAP

◎ Decadent All-Vegetable Soap

This soap has wonderful skin nurturing oils and is perfect for pampering yourself. If you buy nonrefined cocoa butter, the chocolate scent may come through. Add a fragrance oil like raspberry, and it is a fragrant treat!

12 ounces (341g) avocado oil

2 ounces (57g) castor oil

4 ounces (114g) cocoa butter

8 ounces (227g) coconut oil

24 ounces (682g) olive oil

4 ounces (114g) shea butter

20 ounces (568g) distilled water

7.1 ounces (202g) lye

YIELDS 54 OUNCES (1.5KG) OF SOAP

◎ Cocoa Butter Supreme

Not only does this soap condition and moisturize your skin, it also has a wonderful, natural, chocolate scent, due to the cocoa butter. Play off of this fragrance with chocolate-covered cherries soap or caramel scented soap.

2 ounces (57g) castor oil

4 ounces (114g) cocoa butter

12 ounces (341g) coconut oil

12 ounces (341g) grapeseed oil

24 ounces (682g) olive oil

16 ounces (454g) distilled water

7.4 ounces (210g) lye

YIELDS 54 OUNCES (1.5KG) OF SOAP

◎ Shea Soft Soap

This is a great skin softening bar of soap because of the oils used, especially shea butter. You will truly enjoy using this indulgent, creamy bar of soap.

8 ounces (227g) avocado oil

2 ounces (57g) castor oil

10 ounces (284g) coconut oil

24 ounces (682g) olive oil

8 ounces (227g) palm kernel oil

6 ounces (170g) shea butter

22 ounces (624g) distilled water

7.8 ounces (222g) lye

YIELDS 58 OUNCES (1.6KG) OF SOAP

◎ Low-Cost Vegetable Soap

This recipe is economical and the oils are readily available, but it has minimal conditioning oils. For people with dry skin, add some aloe vera juice in place of some of the distilled water. You may also want to add 1/4 cup (60ml) of ground oats to help draw moisture to the skin as it gently exfoliates.

24 ounces (681g) canola oil

2 ounces (57g) castor oil

6 ounces (170g) coconut oil

24 ounces (682g) olive oil

16 ounces (454g) distilled water

7.5 ounces (213g) lye

YIELDS 56 OUNCES (1.6KG) OF SOAP

Lard and Tallow Soaps

⊕ *Simply Soap*

This is a basic soap recipe using lard. With the added castor coconut and palm kernel oils, you will get a mountain of bubbles with this recipe!

> 2 ounces (57g) castor oil
> 16 ounces (454g) coconut oil
> 24 ounces (682g) olive oil
> 8 ounces (227g) palm kernel oil
> 6 ounces (170g) lard
> 21 ounces (596g) distilled water
> 7.8 ounces (222g) lye

YIELDS 56 OUNCES (1.6KG) OF SOAP

⊕ *Down Home & Broke Soap*

The ingredients in this recipe are readily available at most grocers and relatively inexpensive. This is a great recipe for a beginner who is trying out soapmaking for the first time.

> 32 ounces (909g) lard or tallow
> 24 ounces (682g) canola, corn, sunflower, safflower or any combination of these four vegetable oils
> 21 ounces (596g) distilled water
> 7.2 ounces (204g) lye

YIELDS 56 OUNCES (1.6KG) OF SOAP

⊕ *Near Home Soap*

A recipe with larger amounts of lard may produce a stronger soap smell. Use heavier fragrances to scent this recipe such as mixed spices or bay rum.

> 2 ounces (57g) castor oil
> 18 ounces (511g) lard or tallow
> 32 ounces (909g) olive oil
> 20 ounces (568g) distilled water
> 6.6 ounces (187g) lye

YIELDS 52 OUNCES (1.5KG) OF SOAP

What happens when you make a batch of soap and it is too soft? What if it doesn't lather? Why are there white spots in the soap? This section will answer some common questions and tell you how to fix some of the inevitable mistakes.

Q My soap has white specks and hard chunks in it. What have I done wrong?

a There are two common reasons for white specks in hot-process soap. First, the temperature of the soap pot is too hot, and the outside of the soap is cooking faster than the inside. Simply turn down the temperature to get a more uniform cook. Or, another common reason has to do with combining the lye. Make sure your lye is completely dissolved in the water before you add the oils.

Q While the soap is cooking, it starts to stick to the sides of the slow cooker. What is going on?

a The outside of the soap is cooking faster than the inside. Turn the temperature down on your cooker so that the soap cooks consistently.

Q How can I tell if my soap has fully saponified?

a It is easy to determine if hot-process soap has saponified. After approximately 30 minutes, the soap should be a translucent color and have glycerin floating on top of slightly bubbly soap. At this point, stir the soap and it should look like opaque, warm petroleum jelly.

Other soapmakers test for saponification by doing the finger or tongue test. To do the finger test, rub the soap mixture between your pointer finger and thumb. If it feels gritty, the soap mixture has not yet saponified. Allow the soap to cook another 10 minutes and then repeat the rubbing test. When the soap rubs smoothly between your fingers and cools rapidly, the soap is fully saponified. Note: It is possible to have smooth unsaponified soap. To do the tongue test, quickly dab some soap onto your finger and touch it to your tongue. If you feel a slight zing, cook your soap for another 10 minutes.

My soap has been cooking for 10 minutes, and it looks like mashed potatoes. What happened?

a This is common and normal. Your soap has only settled down and flattened out. It is cooking on the sides and on the bottom of the pot. The oils are smoothing out and settling down from the heat. Leave the soap alone and let it continue to cook. After 15–20 minutes the sides should curl like a normal batch of soap.

My soap has gone through saponification, but there is oil floating on top. What have I done wrong?

a Absolutely nothing! Congratulations, your soap has saponified. One of the natural by-products of soap is glycerin, the liquid that is floating on top of your soap. Stir the glycerin back into the soap. Watch as the soap turns more opaque and looks like warmed petroleum jelly.

I started to stir the glycerin back into the soap but there was a hard lump in the middle. What should I do?

a This recipe is not quite finished. Some oils produce more glycerin and they produce it faster than other oils. Let the soap cook for another 10 minutes to finish the saponification process.

I added fragrance oils to my soap, but now that the soap has been molded and cooled, I can't smell the fragrance. Why?

a If there is no fragrance in the soap, you may have added the fragrance oils or essential oils too soon in the soapmaking process. After the soap has saponified, allow the soap to cool down before you add the fragrance. Too much heat can burn off the fragrance or essential oils.

My soap has cracks and bubbles in it after it has been molded. Why does this happen?

a Cracks and bubbles can occur for a number of reasons. You may have forgotten to add an ingredient, or your measurements were inaccurate and you used too much lye. Perhaps the soap cooked too long or wasn't molded properly and began to dry out.

Q **Why won't my soap harden?**

a If after 24 hours your soap is still too soft to unmold, you may have incorrectly measured your ingredients. Check your recipe. You may have used too much water or oils, or too little lye. Also when designing your own recipes, make sure the oils are correctly balanced.

Q **I can't get my soap out of the mold. What has happened and what can I do about it now?**

a Whenever you are adding soap into a mold, make sure you line it with freezer paper or a plastic trash bag or spray it with olive oil. For soap that won't budge from the mold, put it in the freezer. The cold will make the soap contract, making it easier to remove.

Q **I sprayed my log mold but the soap will not come out. How can I get the soap out of the mold?**

a If you experience a suction problem, run a knife along the edges to release some of the pressure. With wooden molds, be sure to always line them with freezer paper—even if the wood has been specially treated—to prevent a suction problem.

Q **My soap curdled. What has happened?**

a This reaction is called seizing. It is a chemical reaction between lye and fragrance oil occurring when the fragrance oil is added before the soap has saponified. Seizing should not be a problem in hot-process soapmaking, because you should always add the fragrance and essential oils after saponification.

Q **I made a recipe that I don't really like. How do I rebatch and start over?**

a When you are making your own recipes, you often learn by trial and error. Sometimes you will produce a wonderful bar of soap. Other times, you will make a batch that is not well balanced. Recycle those batches by shredding the soap with a hand grater. Add 25% shredded soap to 75% of a new recipe 15 minutes into the cook. Cook until it is incorporated into the new recipe, at least 15 more minutes.

Q *I have a marbling effect in the soap. It has swirls or speckles. What is this?*

a In hot-process soapmaking, marbling often occurs when you are making a recipe with butters, especially shea butter, because it is high in unsaponifiables. If the butters haven't traced thick enough, they may begin to separate, causing a marbled effect.

Q *I have active lye in my cured soap. What should I do?*

a First of all, active lye in your soap can be dangerous. You may have measured inaccurately, in which case you need to rebatch. If you experimented with making your own recipe and are unsure if you have calculated the oils, water and lye correctly, it is best to throw the batch away and go back to the drawing board.

Q *My soap is rising really quickly. What do I do?*

a The soap mixture is rising because there is pent-up heat. All you need to do is stir the soap mixture to release some of the heat.

Q *Why did the soap in my pot boil over?*

a Basically there was pent-up heat in the bottom of your pot, and when the heat was released, the soap rose with it and boiled over. There are many reasons why soap can boil over: your pot may be too small for the amount of soap you are making, or the temperature is too high, creating a pent up heat. Remember to carefully monitor your pot as your soap cooks.

Q *I made my own double boiler out of two mismatched pots. The soap is taking a very long time to cook. What is going on?*

a The cooking is taking so long because a lot of water is escaping out as steam. As the water evaporates out of the outside pot, it takes much longer to cook the soap. For the double boiler to make a uniform batch of soap, the heat must remain constant. Keep the water pot on a rolling boil. Also, if you find you are losing too much water in the form of steam, cover the rim of the outside pot with aluminum foil. Keep approximately 1"–1½" (3cm–4cm) of space between the two pots.

Let's experiment! Now that you've learned the basics of soapmaking, you can design your own soap recipes. Perhaps you have a few favorite recipes and now want to create your own personalized bar of soap, specially designed for the needs of your skin. In order to design your own recipes, you do not need a chemistry degree, but you do need to learn the general properties of each oil, how to calculate the amount of lye and water you need and what essential oils blend well together. Once you learn these basics, you will enjoy designing your own recipes for yourself, your family and your friends.

Charts & References

Keep in mind that designing your own recipes is a trial and error process. Your job is to make a bar that is hard enough to not melt quickly and conditioning enough so it won't dry your skin. Use the Charts & References section on pages 110–120 in conjunction with this section to design your own recipes.

Oil Properties Chart

First, look at the Oil Properties Chart on page 110–111. This chart shows the most common oils used in soapmaking. The top of the chart shows the most abundant fatty acids in these oils, as well as the oil's iodine value. Fatty acids are important to soapmaking because they give oils their properties and characteristics. Notice the basics: oleic, linoleic and ricinoleic conditions; lauric, myristic, palmitic and stearic harden and make a full lather (note: ricinoleic also produces a lather). Therefore, the chart lists the percentage amounts of the major fatty acids in the oils. Some oils show a percentage range. For instance, almond oil contains anywhere from 8%– 28% of linoleic acid, depending on the process used to extract the oil. When designing recipes, you have to balance out the fatty acid properties. Let's look a little closer at this chart and the major fatty acids:

• iodine value

Generally you can look in the iodine column of this chart to determine what kind of hardening power each oil has. The lower the number, the harder the bar of soap. Coconut oil, which produces a harder bar, has an iodine value of 10, whereas kukui nut oil, which produces a softer bar, has an iodine range of 155–175. This is true if you are only using one oil in your soap recipe. When you combine oils, you need to consider the properties of each oil to balance enough hardening power with enough conditioning power. As a result of information from this column, soapmakers categorize oils as soap hardening oils, soap softening oils or oils that do not soften or harden the recipe. Note: The exception is castor oil. Even though it has an iodine value of 82–90, it will not harden soap. This value is so high since it contains 90% ricinoleic fatty acids.

• oleic acid

Most of the oleic oils will maintain the hardness in the hard oils (lauric, myristic, palmitic and stearic) and the soft oils (linoleic and ricinoleic). Oleic conditioning is not as noticeable in terms of softening your skin, but it provides a heavier type of conditioning. Bars that have mostly oleic fatty acids often leave a bit of oil on the skin after rinsing, and may take a little longer to dry on your skin.

✳

Tips For Choosing Oils:

- Iodine values indicate if the oil will make a hard or soft bar, except for castor oil.

- When using a large amount of myristic and lauric fatty acids, balance the recipe with a lot of oleic, some linoleic and a touch ricinoleic to replace the skin's natural oil.

- You will need to increase the amount of "hard oils" when using both castor and linoleic oils.

- Oleic fatty acids are neutral.

- Ricinoleic and linoleic soften a bar of soap.

- Palmitic, stearic, lauric and myristic acids harden a bar of soap.

- Butters are high in palmitic, oleic and lineolic acids.

• linoleic acid

As you can tell from the iodine value, this fatty acid has softening power. It provides light skin conditioning and rinses clean. It can also make older skin feel softer and more supple. The higher the percentage of linoleic acids in your recipe, the more softening power you will have. If the other hardening oils in the recipe are not too high, thus overpowering the oleic oils, you can feel the wonderful effects of linoleic fatty acids with as little as 6–8 ounces (170g–227g).

• ricinoleic acid

Ricinoleic acid is the strongest soap softener by far. In small amounts [2–4 ounces (57g–114g) per recipe] it will create mounds of tiny bubbles, add a creamy, lotion-like feel and soften your soap. I do not recommend using any more than 4 ounces (114g) of a ricinoleic oil in a recipe. It will not increase the creamy feel or the suds, and actually will not produce a hard enough bar. Notice on the chart that castor oil is the only oil that contains ricinoleic acid. Because it is so strong (90% ricinoleic), it negates the iodine value that normally determines any particular oil's hardening power.

• lauric and myristic acids

In high amounts, these fatty acids not only give you a harder bar with fluffy lather, but they will feel drying on your skin and can strip your skin of its natural oils. Coconut and palm kernel oils have a high amount of lauric acid and a considerable amount of myristic acid. These fatty acids give soap hardening power, so be sure to counter the effects with all or a combination of oleic, linoleic and ricinoleic conditioning oils in your recipe.

• palmitic and stearic acids

These fatty acids harden soap, but unlike the lauric and myristic fatty acids, they do not strip the skin of its natural oil. Butters and animal fats generally contain the highest amounts of these fatty acids. Palm oil is unique in that it is relatively high in stearic acid, but has hardly any palmitic. As a result, it is a mediocre hardening oil compared to butters and fats.

Lye & Water Calculation Chart

Once you have chosen which oils you would like to use for a recipe, use this chart on page 112 to figure out exactly how much water and lye are needed. The left-hand column shows the most popular oils to use when making soap. Once you have decided how many ounces of an oil you plan to use in a recipe, figure the amount of lye. This chart shows SAP values, or the amount of lye needed for 1, 2, 3 or 4 ounces (28g,

57g, 85g, 113g) of every oil. These figures are calculated to 6% superfat. This means that the soap will have about 6% oil left in it that will not be turned to soap, leaving it more moisturizing and conditioning. All you need to do is add up the amounts of each oil under the appropriate column. If you want to calculate the amount of lye need for 6 ounces (170g), for example, then you simply calculate the amount needed for 2 ounces (57g) and 4 ounces (114g), and add those two figures together.

To figure out the amount of water needed for your recipe, simply use the total amount of ounces of oil required. If that number is less than 16 ounces (454g), then multiply that amount by 0.411. If the ounces of oil needed for the recipe is greater than 32 ounces (909g), multiply that amount by 0.377. Once you have the exact measurements, check your math again and then make your recipe.

Oil Characteristics Guide

This chart on page 113 shows, at a glance, the characteristics of common oils used in soapmaking. It shows two important factors for figuring out which oils to use. First, it lists how well each oil conditions your skin, listing it in a range from 0–10, where 10 represents the most skin conditioning. Secondly, this chart shows how well each oil hardens a bar of soap, ranging from 1–4, where 1 is the hardest and 4 is the softest. If you notice, the oils are listed from hardest (coconut oil) to softest (castor oil). The oils in the middle of the chart are fairly neutral; they neither soften nor harden a bar of soap. The oils are color coded so you can look at this chart and quickly see which oils behave similarly.

Essential Oil Blending Characteristics

This chart, provided in part by A Garden Eastward, is a time and a money saver. It is an excellent resource, providing a comprehensive listing of the most popular and common essential oils. This chart also gives characteristics of the scent, including whether it is a top, middle or base note, and it lists what other oils blend well with each essential oil.

Remember it is always important to sample essential oils before you begin working with them. Essential oils vary in their fragrance depending on a variety of factors. Shop around and work very closely with your fragrance vendor. It is also important to remember that this part of the soapmaking process is entirely subjective. Use this information as a guide but also experiment with fragrance combinations on your own.

Using the Charts to Make a Recipe

The following example walks you through the process of designing you own recipes step by step.

1 Choose the Number of Oils You Want to Use

It is entirely up to you as to how many oils you want to use. Some recipes, like Spanish castile, require only one oil, and other recipes include up to ten. It is your decision. A common rule of thumb is to use four to six oils. Four is the minimum number of oils with different enough characteristics to produce a hard bar, and any more than six oils in a recipe would turn into a very expensive batch of soap! For this example, let's say that we want to use four oils.

2 Decide Which Oils You Want to Use

Again, this is subjective. It is your own personal preference as to which oils you use. Sometimes this decision is based on which oils you have on hand and readily available. You may have very sensitive skin and can only use specific oils. Looking at the Oil Characteristics Guide on page 113, choose oils that offer both hardening and softening power, balanced with skin conditioning qualities. In other words, you would not want to choose all four oils that are all very conditioning and soft because the soap would not have enough hardening power. Likewise, you would not want to pick four oils that have excellent soap hardening qualities because it would produce a hard, drying bar of soap. Balance the oils with a wide range of characteristics. For this example, let's say we chose these four oils:

- coconut oil
- olive oil
- safflower oil
- castor oil

3 Use the Oil Charts to Determine the Characteristics of the Soap

With both the Oil Characteristics Guide plus the Oil Properties Chart on page 110, determine if these four oils can work together to make a conditioning, balanced bar of soap.

Coconut oil will give the soap hardening power while the castor oil is a strong soap softener. Olive oil is a fairly neutral oil, which brings out the qualities of the other oils and would be a nice filler oil. Finally, safflower oil will provide some softening power. Remember that castor oil is high in ricinoleic acid and safflower is high in linoleic acid. While you could balance the recipe to give you enough hardening power, you will have extreme soap softening to counter. I suggest you find another oil in place of safflower to provide some skin conditioning that is not so high in linoleic acid. How about hazelnut instead? Hazelnut oil does not contain as much lineolic acid but provides mild conditioning and may slightly soften the soap. After looking at the charts and identifying these oils, you can determine that they could make a nice recipe, as long as you figure out the appropriate amounts.

4 Ask Yourself Some Key Questions

When figuring out how much of each oil to use, you should ask yourself the following questions:

- How much coconut oil do I need to put in the recipe to keep the bar hard? Then again, because coconut oil dries out your skin when used in high amounts, how much can I use without going overboard?
- How much hazelnut oil can I add so this bar is conditioning but isn't too soft?

- What is the lowest amount of castor oil that I can use to get the conditioning benefits while countering the hardening power of the coconut oil?
- Do these oils balance out the hardening properties with the skin conditioning and soap softening properties?

5 Compare Your Oils With Other Recipes Given in the Book

Look at other recipes in this book to get an idea of how much of each type of oil you should include in your recipe. Do you see the four oils used in the recipe? Or can you see comparable recipes using oils with similar properties?

6 Assign the Amounts of Oil

After looking at other recipes in this book, let's plug in the following values:

- 12 ounces (341g) coconut oil
- 24 ounces (682g) olive oil
- 12 ounces (341g) hazelnut oil
- 2 ounces (57g) castor oil

7 Determine the SAP Value

Using the Lye & Water Calculation Chart on page 112, you will notice that for 1 ounce (28g) of each oil, the SAP values are given. Therefore, the SAP values for the oils used in this recipe are:

- 0.17 for 1 ounce (28g) coconut oil
- 0.13 for 1 ounce (28g) olive oil
- 0.13 for 1 ounce (28g) hazelnut oil
- 0.12 for 1 ounce (28g) castor oil

8 Determine the Amount of Lye

Again, using the Lye & Water Calculation Chart (page 112), multiply the SAP values by the number of ounces required for this recipe. Add all of those amounts up to get the total amount of lye required for saponification.

- 0.17 x 12 ounces (341g) = 2.04 ounces (58g) coconut oil
- 0.13 x 24 ounces (682g) = 3.12 ounces (88g) olive oil
- 0.13 x 12 ounces (341g) = 1.56 ounces (46g) hazelnut oil
- 0.12 x 2 ounces (57g) = 0.24 ounces (7g) castor oil

Therefore, a total of 6.96 ounces (197g) of lye is required for this recipe.

9 Figure the Total Amount of Distilled Water Required for This Recipe

Because this recipe requires more than 32 ounces (909g) of oils, multiply 0.377 by the total amount of oil.

- 50 ounces (1.4kg) x 0.377 = 18.9 ounces (536g) of water

10 Verify Your Results

Check your calculations to make sure that the recipe is accurate.

- 12 ounces (341g) coconut oil
- 24 ounces (682g) olive oil
- 12 ounces (341g) hazelnut oil
- 2 ounces (57g) castor oil
- 6.96 ounces (197g) lye
- 18.9 ounces (536g) distilled water

Congratulations! You have successfully created your own recipe. Choose the fragrances, colorants and other additives of your choice.

Charts & References

Oil Properties Chart

This chart provides information on fatty acids, which is helpful in determining which oils to combine in a recipe to make a conditioning, yet hard bar of soap. This chart also gives the saponification values per 1 ounce (28g) for commonly used oils.

OIL PROPERTIES CHART

Fatty Acid — What does this oil do?	Lauric — Hard bar, Fluffy lather, In high amounts strips natural skin oils	Myristic — Hard bar, Fluffy lather, In high amounts strips natural skin oils	Linoleic — Conditions, Rinses clean, Softens soap in higher amounts	Oleic — Conditions	Palmitic — Hardens bar, Stable lather	Ricinoleic — Creamy lather and conditions, Very strong soap softener	Stearic — Hardens bar, Stable lather	Iodine — The lower the number, the harder the bar except for Castor
Almond*			8-28%	64-82%	6-8%			93-106
Andiroba			9%	51%	28%		8%	
Apricot Kernel			20-34%	58-74%	4-7%			92-108
Argan			32%	47%	14%		6%	
Avocado			6-18%	36-80%	7-32%		2%	80-95
Babassu	50%	20%		10%	11%		4%	10-20
Black Currant/Cassis			47-48%	9-11%	6%		2%	
Borage			30-40%	15-20%	9-12%		3-4%	
Canola/Rapeseed			22%	60%	4%		2%	105-120
Castor			3-4%	3-4%		90%		82-90
Cocoa Butter			3%	34-36%	25-30%		31-35%	33-42
Coconut*	39-54%	15-23%	1-2%	4-11%	6-11%		1-4%	<10
Corn			45-56%	28-37%	12-14%		2-3%	103-130
Cottonseed			52%	18%	13%		13%	80
Emu		0.4%	14%	50%	21%		9%	75
Evening Primrose			65-80%	6-11%	7%		2%	
Flax/Linseed			7-19%	14-39%	4-9%		2-4%	105-115
Grapeseed			58-78%	12-28%	5-11%		3-6%	125-142
Hazelnut*			7-11%	65-85%	4-6%		1-4%	90-103
Hemp			57%	12%	6%		2%	167

Fatty Acid	Lauric	Myristic	Linoleic	Oleic	Palmitic	Ricinoleic	Stearic	Iodine
Jojoba				10-13%				80-85
Kukui Nut*			42%	20%	6%			155-175
Lard		1%	6%	46%	28%		13%	43
Macadamia Nut*			1-3%	54-63%	7-10%		2-6%	73-79
Mango Butter			1-13%	34-56%	3-18%		26-57%	55-65
Neem			13%	50%	18%		15%	84-94
Olive			5-15%	63-81%	7-14%		3-5%	79-95
Ostrich	0.03%	0.85%	2%	38%	26%		6%	
Palm			9-11%	38-40%	43-45%		4-5%	45-57
Palm Kernel	47%	14%		18%	9%			37
Peach Kernel			15-35%	55-75%	5-8%			108-118
Peanut*			32%	45%	10%		2%	
Rapeseed/Canola			15%	32%	1%			105-120
Rice Bran			32-47%	32-38%	13-23%		2-3%	105-115
Safflower			70-80%	10-20%	6-7%			86-119
Safflower–High Oleic			14%	75%	4%		2%	92
Sesame			39-47%	37-42%	8-11%		4-6%	105-115
Shea Butter			3-8%	40-55%	3-7%		36-45%	55-71
Soy			46-53%	21-27%	9-12%		4-6%	124-132
Sunflower			70%	16%	7%		4%	119-138
Sunflower–High Oleic			4%	83%	3%		4%	83
Tallow, beef		3-6%	2-3%	37-43%	24-32%		20-25%	42-45
Walnut*			54-65%	14-21%	6-8%		1-3%	140-150
Wheat Germ			55-60%	13-21%	13-20%		2%	125-135

*Note: Anyone with nut allergies should avoid using these oils.

Lye and Water Calculation Chart

After you have determined which oils to use in a recipe that will produce a balanced bar of soap, you must determine the amount of lye and water for the recipe. Use this chart and individually calculate the amount of lye required to saponify each oil. Then add that amount to figure the total amount of lye. To figure the amount of water, add the ounces of oil used. If that amount is less than 16 ounces (480ml), multiply that amount by 0.411. If the total ounces of oil is great than 16 ounces (480ml), multiply that amount by 0.377. The figures are calculated to 6% superfat, which basically means that there is going to be a slight amount of leftover oil that will not be saponified. This is done so that the soap does not contain active lye as well as provides additional conditioning.

Common Oils	1 oz. oil needs this much lye	2 oz. oil needs this much lye	3 oz. oil needs this much lye	4 oz. oil needs this much lye	Common Oils	1 oz. oil needs this much lye	2 oz. oil needs this much lye	3 oz. oil needs this much lye	4 oz. oil needs this much lye
Almond	0.13	0.26	0.52	1.04	Lard	0.13	0.26	0.52	1.04
Apricot Kernel	0.13	0.26	0.51	1.02	Macadamia Nut	0.13	0.26	0.52	1.05
Avocado	0.13	0.25	0.5	0.98	Mango Butter	0.13	0.25	0.5	1.01
Canola	0.13	0.26	0.51	1.03	Olive	0.13	0.26	0.51	1.02
Castor	0.12	0.24	0.48	0.96	Palm	0.13	0.26	0.53	1.04
Cocoa Butter	0.13	0.26	0.51	1.03	Palm Kernel	0.15	0.29	0.6	1.18
Coconut	0.17	0.35	0.69	1.38	Rice Bran	0.13	0.25	0.5	1.01
Corn	0.13	0.26	0.51	1.02	Safflower–High Linoleic	0.13	0.25	0.5	1.01
Cottonseed	0.13	0.26	0.52	1.04	Shea Butter	0.12	0.24	0.48	0.96
Emu	0.13	0.26	0.52	1.03	Soy	0.13	0.26	0.51	1.02
Evening Primrose	0.13	0.26	0.51	1.02	Sunflower–High Linoleic	0.13	0.26	0.51	1.03
Grapeseed	0.13	0.26	0.5	1.0	Tallow, beef	0.13	0.26	0.53	1.06
Hazelnut	0.13	0.26	0.52	1.04	Tallow, sheep/goat	0.13	0.26	0.53	1.06
Jojoba	0.06	0.12	0.26	0.5	Walnut	0.13	0.26	0.51	1.02
					Wheat Germ	0.13	0.25	0.5	1.01
Less Common Oils					Kukui Nut	0.13	0.26	0.51	1.03
Borage	0.13	0.26	0.51	1.02	Lanolin	0.07	0.14	0.28	0.56
Flax/Linseed	0.13	0.26	0.51	1.03	Neem	0.13	0.26	0.51	1.03
Hemp	0.13	0.52	0.52	1.03	Peanut	0.13	0.26	0.51	1.02

To calculate water for recipe using oil weight	Multiply oil weight by this percentage	Example
≤16 ounces (28.35g)	0.411	**oil weight = 54oz. (1530.87g)**
≥32 ounces (57.7g)	0.377	54 × 0.377 = 20.35 oz. water 1530.87 × 0.377 = 576.91g water

Oil Characteristics Guide

This chart is helpful when determining which oils to combine when making your own recipe. The oils listed in each color-coded section are interchangeable in your soap recipe.

Oil or Fat	Conditioning Scale 0=Least 5=Mild 10=Most	Hardness Scale 1=Hardens soap 2=Maintains hardness 3=Not much effect 4=Softens soap	Oil or Fat	Conditioning Scale 0=Least 5=Mild 10=Most	Hardness Scale 1=Hardens soap 2=Maintains hardness 3=Not much effect 4=Softens soap
Coconut	2	1	Avocado	9	3
Palm Kernel	2	1	Apricot Kernel	5	2
Cocoa Butter	7	1	Canola	4	2
Lard	5	1	Corn	2	3
Tallow	6	1	Evening Primrose	6	3
Palm	4	1-2	Hazelnut	6	2-3
Emu Oil	10	1-2	Rice Bran	4	3
Shea Butter	9	1-2	Grapeseed	6	4
Mango Butter	7	1-2	Safflower	7	4
Macadamia Nut	7	1-2	Sunflower	7	4
Cottonseed	0	1-2	Soy	2	4
Jojoba	6	1-2	Wheat Germ	6	3-4
Olive	5	1-2	Walnut	6	3-4
Almond	6	2	Castor	9	4

Essential Oil Blending Characteristics

This comprehensive chart provides detailed information on the most commonly used essential oils. Use this chart when blending essential oils. It gives information on which fragrances blend well together and whether the oil is a top, middle or base note.

Essential Oil	Characteristics	Perfume Note	Blends Well With
Allspice	Leaf: Powerful sweet-spicy. Berry: Sweet, warm, balsamic-spicy middle note and fresh, clean top note.	Middle to top	Ginger, Geranium, Lavender, Opopanax, Labdanum, Ylang Ylang, Patchouli, Neroli, Oriental, Spices
Ambrette Seed	Rich, sweet, floral-musky odor, very tenacious	Middle	Rose, Neroli, Sandalwood, Clary Sage, Cypress, Patchouli, Oriental Bases
Angelica	Root: Rich herbaceous-earthy. Seed: fresh, spicy	Top	Patchouli, Clary Sage, Oakmoss, Vetiver, Citrus
Basil	Light, fresh, sweet-spicy; balsamic undertone	Top	Bergamot, Clary Sage, Lime, Opopanax, Oakmoss, Citronella, Geranium, Hyssop, "green" notes
Bergamot	Fresh, sweet-fruity, slightly spicy-balsamic undertone	Top	Lavender, Neroli, Jasmine, Cypress, Geranium, Lemon, Chamomile, Juniper, Coriander, Violet
Cabreuva	Sweet, woody-floral, very delicate with great tenacity	Base	Rose, Cassie, Mimosa, Cedarwood, Woody, Oriental
Cajeput	Penetrating, camphoraceous-medicinal	Top	Lavandin, Lavender, Clary Sage, Rosemary, Oakmoss, Pine, Cananga, Geranium, Margoram, Spices
Calendula	Intensely sharp, herbaceous	Middle	Oakmoss, Hyacinth, Florals, Citrus
Camphor	Sharp, pungent, camphoraceous	Top	Frankincense, Ylang Ylang, Orange, Mandarin
Caraway	Strong, warm, sweet-spicy	Middle	Jasmine, Cinnamon, Spices
Cardamom	Sweet-spicy, warm; woody-balsamic undertone	Top	Rose, Frankincense, Orange, Bergamot, Cinnamon, Cloves, Caraway, Ylang Ylang, Labdanum, Cedarwood, Neroli, Oriental

Essential Oil	Characteristics	Perfume Note	Blends Well With
Carrot Seed	Warm, dry, woody-earthy	Middle	Costus, Cassie, Mimosa, Cedarwood, Geranium, Citrus, Spice
Catnip	Herbaceous-woody, pungent	Middle	
Cedarwood	Warm, camphoraceous top note: sweet, tenacious, woody-balsamic undertone	Base	Rosewood, Bergamot, Cypress, Cassie, Jasmine, Juniper, Neroli, Mimosa, Labdanum, Frankincense, Clary Sage, Vetiver, Rosemary, Ylang Ylang, Oriental, Floral
Celery Seed	Spicy-warm and sweet	Top/Middle	Lavender, Pine, Opopanax, Lovage, Tea
Chamomile, German	Strong, sweetish, warm-herbaceous	Middle	Geranium, Lavender, Patchouli, Rose, Benzoin, Neroli, Bergamot, Marjoram, Lemon, Ylang Ylang, Jasmine, Clary Sage, Labdanum
Chamomile, Roman	Warm, sweet, fruity-herbaceous	Middle	Bergamot, Clary Sage, Oakmoss, Jasmine, Labdanum, Neroli, Rose, Geranium, Lavender
Cinnamon	Sweet, warm-spicy, dry, tenacious	Middle	Frankincense, Ylang Ylang, Orange, Mandarin, Benzoin, Peru balsam, Oriental
Citronella	Fresh, lemony, woody-sweet	Top	Geranium, Lemon, Bergamot, Orange, Cedarwood, Pine
Copaiba Balsam	Mild, sweet, balsamic-peppery	Base	Cananga, Ylang Ylang, Vanilla, Jasmine, Violet, Florals
Coriander	Sweet, woody-spicy, slightly musky	Top	Clary Sage, Bergamot, Jasmine, Frankincense, Neroli, Petitgrain, Citronella, Sandalwood, Cypress, Pine, Ginger, Spices
Cumin	Warm, soft, spicy-musky	Top	Lavender, Lavandin, Rosemary, Galbanum, Rosewood, Cardamom, Oriental
Cypress	Smoky, sweet-balsamic, tenacious	Middle	Cedarwood, Pine, Lavender, Mandarin, Clary Sage, Lemon, Cardamom, Moroccan, Chamomile, Ambrette Seed, Labdanum, Juniper, Benzoin, Bergamot, Margoram, Orange, Sandalwood

Essential Oil	Characteristics	Perfume Note	Blends Well With
Dill	Seed: Light, fresh, warm-spicy; Herb: Powerful, sweet-spicy	Middle	Elemi, Mint, Caraway, Nutmeg, Spice, Citrus
Elemi	Light, fresh, balsamic-spicy, lemon-like	Base/Middle	Myrrh, Frankincense, Labdanum, Rosemary, Lavender, Lavandin, Sage, Cinnamon, Spices
Eucalyptus	Somewhat harsh, camphoraceous; woody-scent undertone	Top	Thyme, Rosemary, Lavender, Marjoram, Pine, Cedarwood, Lemon
Eucalyptus, Lemon	Strong, fresh, citronella-like; sweet, balsamic undertone	Top	Thyme, Rosemary, Lavender, Marjoram, Pine, Cedarwood, Lemon
Fennel, Sweet	Very sweet, anise-like, slightly earthy-peppery	Top/Middle	Geranium, Lavender, Rose, Sandalwood
Fir Needle	Pleasing, rich, sweet-balsamic	Middle	Galbanum, Labdanum, Lavender, Rosemary, Lemon, Pine, Marjoram
Frankincense	Fresh, terpeney top note; warm, rich, sweet-balsamic undertone	Base	Sandalwood, Pine, Vetiver, Geranium, Lavender, Mimosa, Neroli, Orange, Bergamot, Camphor, Basil, Pepper, Cinnamon, Spices
Galbanum	Fresh, green top note; Woody-dry balsamic undertone	Middle	Hyacinth, Violet, Narcissus, Lavender, Geranium, Oakmoss, Opopanax, Pine, Fir, Styrax, Oriental
Geranium	Rosey-sweet, minty	Middle to Top	Lavender, Patchouli, Clove, Rose, Neroli, Sandalwood, Jasmine, Juniper, Citrus
Grapefruit	Fresh, sweet, citrus	Top	Lemon, Palmarosa, Bergamot, Neroli, Rosemary, Cypress, Lavender, Geranium, Spices
Guaiacwood	Pleasant, tea-rose-type	Middle	Geranium, Neroli, Oakmoss, Rose, Sandalwood, Spice, Woody-Floral
Helichrysum	Powerful, rich, honey-like, delicate tea-like undertone	Middle	Chamomile, Boronia, Labdanum, Lavender, Mimosa, Oakmoss, Geranium, Clary Sage, Rose, Peru balsam, Clove, Citrus

Essential Oil	Characteristics	Perfume Note	Blends Well With
Hops	Rich, spicy-sweet	Middle	Pine, Hyacinth, Nutmeg, Copaiba, Balsam, Citrus, Spice
Hyssop	Sweet, camphoraceous top note; warm spicy-herbaceous undertone	Middle	Lavender, Rosemary, Myrtle, Bay, Sage, Clary Sage, Geranium, Citrus
Jasmine	Intensely rich, warm, floral, tea-like undertone	Base	Rose, Sandalwood, Clary Sage, Citrus, virtually all oils
Juniper	Berry: Sweet, fresh, woody-balsamic; Needles and wood: Sweet-balsamic, fresh, turpentine-like	Middle	Vetiver, Sandalwood, Cedarwood, Mastic, Oakmoss, Galbanum, Elemi, Cypress, Clary Sage, Pine, Lavender, Lavandin, Labdanum, Fir Needle, Rosemary, Benzoin, Balsam Tolu, Geranium, Citrus
Labdanum	Warm, sweet, dry-herbaceous, musky	Base	Oakmoss, Clary Sage, Pine, Juniper, Calamus, Opopanax, Lavender, Lavandin, Bergamot, Cypress, Vetiver, Sandalwood, Patchouli, Frankincense, Chamomile, Maroc, Oriental
Laurel Leaf	Powerful, spicy-medicinal	Middle	Pine, Cypress, Juniper, Clary Sage, Rosemary, Frankincese, Labdanum, Lavender, Citrus, Spice
Lavandin	Fresh, camphoraceous top note; woody herbaceous undertone	Top/Middle	Clove, Bay, Cinnamon, Citronella, Cypress, Pine, Clary Sage, Geranium, Thyme, Patchouli, Rosemary, Citrus
Lavender	Sweet, floral-herbaceous; balsamic-woody undertone	Top/Middle	Most oils
Lemon	Light, fresh, citrus	Top	Lavender, Neroli, Ylang Ylang, Rose, Sandalwood, Frankincense, Chamomile, Benzoin, Fennel, Geranium, Eucalyptus, Juniper, Oakmoss, Lavandin, Elemi, Labdanum, Citrus
Lemon Balm	Light, fresh, lemony	Top	Lavender, Geranium, Florals, Citrus
Lemongrass	Fresh, grassy-citrus; earthy undertone	Top	Lavender, Neroli, Ylang Ylang, Rose, Sandalwood, Frankincense, Chamomile, Benzoin, Fennel, Geranium, Eucalyptus, Juniper, Oakmoss, Lavandin, Elemi, Labdanum, Citrus
Lime	Fresh, sweet, citrus-peel	Top	Neroli, Citronella, Lavender, Lavandin, Rosemary, Clary Sage, Citrus

Essential Oil	Characteristics	Perfume Note	Blends Well With
Lovage	Root-like, rich, spicy-warm, sweet floral undertone	Middle	Rose, Galbanum, Costus, Opopanax, Oakmoss, Bay, Lavandin, Spice
Mandarin	Intensely sweet, almost floral, citrus	Top	Citrus, Spice
Marjoram	Warm, woody, spicy-camphoraceous	Middle	Cedarwood, Pine, Chamomile, Valerian, Vetiver, Oakmoss
Milfoil	Fresh, green, sweet-herbaceous, slightly camphoraceous	Middle	Cedarwood, Pine, Chamomile, Valerian, Vetiver, Oakmoss
Mimosa	Slightly green, woody-floral	Middle	Lavandin, Lavender, Ylang Ylang, Violet, Styrax, Citronella, Peru balsam, Florals, Spices
Myrrh	Warm, sweet-balsamic, slightly spicy-medicinal	Base	Frankincense, Sandalwood, Benzoin, Oakmoss, Cypress, Juniper, Mandarin, Geranium, Patchouli, Thyme, Mints, Lavender, Pine, Spices
Myrtle	Clear, fresh, camphoraceous, sweet-herbaceous	Middle	Bergamot, Lavandin, Lavender, Rosemary, Clary Sage, Hyssop, Bay, Lime, Laurel, Ginger, Clove, Spices
Neroli	Fresh, delicate, rich, warm, sweet-herbaceous	Middle	Most oils, especially Chamomile, Coriander, Geranium, Benzoin, Clary Sage, Jasmine, Lavender, Rose, Ylang Ylang, Citrus
Niaouli	Sweet, fresh, camphoraceous	Top	Lavandin, Lavender, Clary Sage, Rosemary, Oakmoss, Pine, Cananga, Geranium, Marjoram, Spices
Nutmeg	Sweet, warm-spicy, terpeney top note	Middle	Oakmoss, Lavandin, Bay, Peru balsam, Orange, Geranium, Clary Sage, Rosemary, Lime, Petitgrain, Mandarin, Coriander, Spice
Orange, Sweet	Sweet, fresh-fruity	Top	Lavender, Neroli, Lemon, Clary Sage, Myrrh, Spices
Palmarosa	Sweet, floral, rosy, geranium-like	Middle	Cananga, Geranium, Oakmoss, Rosewood, Amyris, Sandalwood, Guaiacwood, Cedarwood, Florals

Essential Oil	Characteristics	Perfume Note	Blends Well With
Peppermint	Highly penetrating, grassy-minty, camphoraceous	Middle	Benzoin, Rosemary, Lavender, Marjoram, Lemon, Eucalyptus, Mints
Peru Balsam	Rich, sweet, vanilla-like	Base	Ylang Ylang, Patchouli, Petitgrain, Sandalwood, Rose, Spices, Florals, Orientals
Petitgrain	Fresh-floral, citrus; woody-herbaceous undertone	Top	Rosemary, Lavender, Geranium, Bergamot, Bitter Orange, Neroli, Labdanum, Oakmoss, Clary Sage, Jasmine, Benzoin, Palmarosa, Clove, Balsams
Rosewood	Very sweet, woody-floral, spicy hint	Top/Middle	Most oils, especially citrus, woods and florals
Spearmint	Warm, spicy-herbaceous, minty	Middle	Lavender, Lavandin, Jasmine, Eucalyptus, Basil, Rosemary, Peppermint
Spike Lavender	Penetrating, fresh-herbaceous, camphoraceous	Middle	Rosemary, Sage, Lavandin, Eucalyptus, Rosewood, Lavender, Petitgrain, Pine, Cedarwood, Oakmoss, Patchouli, Spice
Spikenard	Heavy, sweet-woody, spicy-animal	Middle	Labdanum, Lavender, Oakmoss, Patchouli, Pine Needle, Vetiver, Spices
Star Anise	Warm, spicy, extremely sweet, licorice-like	Middle	Rose, Lavender, Orange, Pine, Spices
Styrax	Sweet-balsamic, rich, tenacious	Base/Middle	Ylang Ylang, Jasmine, Mimosa, Rose, Lavender, Carnation, Violet, Cassie, Spice
Tea Tree	Warm, fresh, spicy-camphoraceous	Top	Lavandin, Lavender, Clary Sage, Rosemary, Oakmoss, Pine, Canaga, Geranium, Marjoram, Spices
Tolu Balsam	Sweet-floral, peppery undertone	Base	Mimosa, Ylang Ylang, Sandalwood, Labdanum, Neroli, Patchouli, Cedarwood, Oriental, Spice, Floral
Ylang Ylang	Intensely sweet, soft, floral-balsamic, slightly spicy	Base/Middle	Most oils, especially Rosewood, Jasmine, Vetiver, Opopanax, Bergamot, Mimosa, Cassie, Peru balsam, Rose, Tuberose, Costus

CONVERSION CHART

To Convert	To	Multiply By
inches	centimeters	2.54
centimeters	inches	0.4
feet	centimeters	30.5
centimeters	feet	0.03
yards	meters	0.9
meters	yards	1.1
square inches	square centimeters	6.45
square centimeters	square inches	0.16
square feet	square meters	0.09
square meters	square feet	10.8
square yards	square meters	0.8
square meters	square yards	1.2
pounds	kilograms	0.45
kilograms	pounds	2.2
ounces	grams	28.4
grams	ounces	0.04
fluid ounces	milliliters	29.57
milliliters	fluid ounces	0.034

Glossary

Active Lye - before the oils, distilled water and lye saponify. Active lye can cause burns.

Animal Fats - tallow, lard and emu oil. Often used with lye and distilled water in the production of soap. Animal fats are generally inexpensive and help produce a harder bar of soap.

Base Oils - a nonfragranced oil that is used to make up the bulk or body of the soap.

Cold Process - soapmaking method where saponification takes place in the molds several weeks to months after combining oils, distilled water and lye.

Color Additives - oxides, ultramarines and FD&C colorants used in soapmaking. They are synthetics used to color soap mixtures.

Digital Scale - a scale that shows weight in numbers rather than a moving needle. This type of scale is more accurate.

Essential Oil – a fragrant oil derived from plant root, stem, petals or leaves. Many have medicinal and/or mood altering properties. Some have precautions against use with certain conditions (ie, pregnancy or allergies) or on some animals. Please read up on the precautions prior to use.

FD&C Colorants - heat stable additives added during tracing. They are unpredictable and can change color throughout the process.

Fragrance Oil - a synthetic fragrance oil that mimics the more expensive natural essential oils. They are produced together in labs and may be totally or partially synthetic.

Glycerin - a liquid produced during saponification.

Hot Process - soapmaking method involving a heat source. Saponification takes place while the mixture cooks.

Lye - sodium hydroxide, caustic soda. An alkaline substance used to saponify oils and water into soap.

Noncomedogenic - will not clog pores.

Oxides - inorganic, heat stable color additives available in black, brown, green, orange and white. They are added when the soap mixture is tracing.

Rebatching - recycling a batch of soap that may have not turned out as expected. Add 25% shredded soap to 75% of a new recipe 15 minutes into the cook. Cook until it is incorporated into the new recipe.

SAP Value - saponification value. The value applied to oils, used to determine how much lye is required to saponify the oil into soap.

Sodium Hydroxide - see Lye.

Saponification - the chemical reaction when oils or fats, distilled water and lye combine. The result is soap.

Seizing - common in cold-process soapmaking, a reaction between lye and fragrance oil. Seizing should not occur during hot-process soapmaking because you should add the fragrance after saponification, when there is no longer lye present in the soap mixture.

Stick Blender - a handheld electric appliance, 12"-16" (30cm–41cm) tall with a stainless steel blade used for mixing small amounts of liquids.

Superfat - to leave oil in a soap recipe to create a milder soap, to prevent lye-heavy creations. For example, using a recipe calculator, you may choose 0% oil left in, or you may choose to leave in a percentage of oil that is not turned to soap for a milder bar. If you chose 5% next to the amount of lye, you are leaving 5% of the oils unsaponified.

Trace - to stir, or stick blend oils, water and lye until it begins to thicken. One can drip the soap solution on top of the mixture and the design remains.

Ultramarines - synthetic color additives that are not heat stable. They are available in a variety of colors.

AUTHOR'S INTERNET GROUP FOR SOAPMAKING
http://groups.yahoo.com/group/HotSoap
Etc

AQUARIUS AROMATHERAPY & SOAP
http://aquariusaroma-soap.com
U.S. Mailing Address:
    P.O. Box 2971
    Sumas, WA 98295-2971
International Mailing Address:
    #31, 32929 Mission Way
    Mission, British Columbia, Canada
    V2V 6E4
    (604) 826-4199
    (604) 826-3322 fax
• supplier of fragrance and essential oils, soap kits and molds

AROMAPEDIA SOFTWARE
www.aromapedia.com
• Internet essential oil database

AROMATHERAPY TODAY
www.aromatherapytoday.com
P. O. Box 211
Kellyville, NSW 2155
Australia
+61 2 9894 9933
+61 2 9894 0199 fax
• information and links on aromatherapy

BOSTON JOJOBA COMPANY
www.bostonjojoba.com
P.O. Box 771
Middleton, MA 01949
(800) 256-5622
• online supplier of jojoba

BRAMBLE BERRY, INC.
www.brambleberry.com
1208 Bay St. Suite C
Bellingham, WA 98225
(360) 734-8278
(360) 752-0992 fax
• supplier of fragrance oils, colorants, kits and molds

CAMDEN-GREY ESSENTIAL OILS
www.essentialoil.net/shop.htm
7178-A SW 47th St.
Miami, FL 33155
(877) 232-7662
(305) 740-3494
(305) 740-8242
• essential oil supplier

CASH & CARRY
www.smartandfinal.com
See Smart & Final Inc.
• foodservice and warehouse grocery company

CHEF'S
www.chefscatalog.com
P.O. Box 620048
Dallas, TX 75262
(800) 884-CHEF
(972) 401-6400 fax
• supplier of kitchen appliances and equipment for soapmaking

COLUMBUS FOODS COMPANY
www.columbusfoods.com
730 N. Albany
Chicago, IL 61612
(800) 322-6457
(773) 265-6985 fax
• base oils, melt & pour base soaps and bulk oils

EMU RANCH LISTINGS FOR U.S., CANADA AND AUSTRALIA
www.emuoilcanada.com/emupeople.html
• emu oil supplier

EMU OIL COMPANY AND POINSETTIA SOAPWORKS
www.gosoap.bizland.com/
theemuoilcompany
• emu oil supplier

THE FUNNERY
94-547 Ukee #303
Waipahu, HI 96797
(808) 677-7852
• soapmaking supplier

A GARDEN EASTWARD
http://addy.com/brinkley/index.html
Ludowici, Georgia 31316
(912) 545-8896
• supplier of base oils, colorants, fragrance and essential oils

GLASPAK INDUSTRIES, INC.
www.glaspak.com/bottles.htm
P.O. Box 8712
Coral Springs, FL 33075
(954) 984-4527
(954) 984-4567 fax
• supplier of glass jars and containers

GLENBROOK FARMS HERBS & SUCH
www.glenbrookfarm.com/herbs/index.htm
7817 193rd Rd.
Live Oak, FL 32060
(888) 716-7627
(386) 362-6481 fax
• supplier of additives, essential oils and fragrance oils

HOLLY HOBBY
www.hollyhobby.com
11582 W. Holly St.
Avondale, AZ 85323
(800) 474-3579
(623) 936-9417 fax
• supplier of molds, fragrance oils, base soaps, soap cutter and tools

LA NATURALE HANDCRAFTED SOAPS LTD.
www.lanaturale.com
1 Station Plaza
Lynbrook, N.Y. 11563
(516) 536-1190
• retailer of handcrafted soaps

THE LEBERMUTH COMPANY, INC.
www.lebermuth.com
P.O. Box 4103B
South Bend, IN 46634
(800) 648-1123
(800) 852-4722 fax
• supplier of fragrance and essential oils and additives

LIBERTY NATURAL PRODUCTS
www.libertynatural.com
8120 SE Stark
Portland, OR 97215
(800) 289-8427
(503) 256-1182 fax
• supplier of essential and fragrance oils, herbs and additives as well as soap

MARTIN CREATIVE
www.martincreative.com
P.O. Box 101
Black Creek, B.C.
V9J 1K8
(250) 337-2237
(250) 337-5117 fax
• supplier of molds

METRIC CONVERSIONS
www.sciencemadesimple.com/
conversions.html
• online measurement converter

MILKY WAY MOLDS, INC.
www.milkywaysoapmolds.com
4326 SE Woodstock
Portland, OR 97206
(800) 588-7930
(360) 665-5907 fax
• supplier of plastic molds for soapmaking
  and candlemaking

MILLER'S SOAP MAKER RESOURCE PAGE
www.silverlink.net/~timer/soapinfo.html
• soapmaking info and recipes

MONTEREY BAY SPICE COMPANY
www.herbco.com/homeindex.htm
719 Swift St., Suite 106
Santa Cruz, CA 95060
(800) 500-6148
(831) 426-2792 fax
• supplier of essential and fragrance oils
  and other herbal additives

NATIONAL CRAFT ASSOCIATION (NCA)
www.craftassoc.com
2012 E. Ridge Rd., Suite 120
Rochester, NY 14622-2434
(800) 715-9594
(716) 785-3231 fax
• information and resources for profes-
  sional crafters

NATURE'S GIFT
www.naturesgift.com
314 Old Hickory Blvd. East
Madison, TN 37115
(615) 612-4270
• essential oil information and warnings

NEILSEN SOAPWERKS
http://soapwerks.com
P.O. Box 742
Siletz, OR 97380
(541) 444-1230
• supplier of molds and instructional
  videos

OLIVE TREE SOAPS
www.olivetreesoaps.com
6190 Stid Hill Rd.
Naples, NY 14512
(716) 374-8052
• handcrafted soap supplier

OREGON TRAIL SOAPS AND SOAPER'S SUPPLY
http://oregontrailsoaps.com
P.O. Box 2115
Rogue River, OR 97537
(541) 582-8995
(541) 582-2046 fax
• supplier of additives, colorants, oils, fragrance oils and melt & pour supplies

OUTBACK EMUZING RANCH
www.emuoilcanada.com/outback.html
RR 2   Site 235   C-12
Courtenay, BC, Canada
V9N 5M9
(866) 338-8227
(250) 338-1108
• emu oil supplier

POYA NATURALS
www.poyanaturals.com
United States:
   2129 Watercress Pl.
   San Ramon, CA 94583
   (800) 246-7817
   (800) 246-8207 fax
Canada:
   21-B Regan Rd.
   Brampton, Ontario L7A 1C5 Canada
   (905) 840-5459
   (905) 846-1784 fax
   (877) 255-7692 order desk
Australia:
   153 Bridge Rd., Glebe,
   Sydney NSW 2037 Australia
   (02) 9566 1900
   (02) 9566 1966 fax
• supplier of essential and fragrance oils

PRECISION CRAFT
www.precisioncraft.net
P.O. Box 486
Brightwood, OR 97011
(503) 622-4544
• supplier of custom-designed molds

RAINBOW MEADOW, INC.
www.rainbowmeadow.com
P.O. Box 457
Napoleon, MI 49261
(800) 207-4047
(517) 817-0025 fax
• supplier of essential oils and raw materials

SAN FRANCISCO HERB CO.
www.sfherb.com
250 14th St.
San Francisco, CA 94103
(800) 227-4530
(415) 861-4440 fax
• supplier of essential and fragrance oils,
  herbal additives and extracts

THE SCENT SHACK
www.thescentshack.com
10 W. State St. #107
Geneva, IL 60134
(630) 845-8931
• soapmaking supplier and information on
  soap conventions

SELF ESSENTIALS
www.selfessentials.com
8140 Industrial Pkwy. #11
Sacramento, CA 95824
(916) 388-9575
(916) 388-9510 fax
• wholesale soapmaking supplier and cosmetic ingredients

SHAW MUDGE & COMPANY
www.shawmudge.com
828 Bridgeport Ave.
Shelton, CT 06484
(203) 925-5000
(203) 925-5098 fax
• fragrance oil supplier

SHAY & COMPANY, INC.
www.shayandcompany.com
7941 SE Steele St., Suite #2
Portland, OR 97206
(503) 775-3420
(503) 775-3486 fax
• distributor of soapmaking supplies and
  cooking oils

SIMPLE PLEASURES
http://members.aol.com/pigmntlady
P.O. Box 194
Old Saybrook, CT 06475
(860) 395-0085 phone/fax
• supplier of cosmetic-grade colorants

SMART & FINAL INC.
www.smartandfinal.com
• foodservice and warehouse grocery
  company

SOAPBERRY LANE
www.soapberrylane.com
P.O. Box 65551
Virginia Beach, VA 23467
(757) 490-8852 phone/fax
• supplier of soapmaking kits, oils, melt &
pour supplies as well as instruction on
cold-process, hand-milled and melt &
pour soapmaking

SOAP SALOON
www.soapsaloon.com
5710 Auburn Blvd. #2
Sacramento, CA. 95841
(916) 334-4894
(916) 334-4897 fax
• supplier of soap molds and soapmaking
supplies

SOAP WIZARDS
www.soapwizards.com
120 E. Main St.
Glenville, MN 56036
(877) 642-3783
(507) 448-2753
• supplier of glycerin melt & pour supplies
as well as other soapmaking supplies

SPECIALTY BOTTLE SUPPLY
www.specialtybottle.com
2730 First Ave. South
Seattle, WA 98134
(206) 340-0459
(206) 903-0785 fax
• supplier of glass and plastic bottles, jars
and containers

STARRVILLE SOAP SUPPLIES
www.starrvillesoapworks.com
6180 Hwy. 271
Tyler, TX 75707
(903) 533-0199
• soapmaking and candlemaking supplier

SUGAR PLUM SUNDRIES
www.sugarplum.net
1715 East Main St.
Chattanooga, TN 37404
(423) 624-4511
• supplier of handcrafted soap, as well as
supplies, recipes and software

SUNBURST BOTTLE COMPANY
www.sunburstbottle.com
5710 Auburn Blvd., Suite 7
Sacramento, CA 95841
(916) 348-5576
(916) 348-3803 fax
• supplier of glass, plastic colored jars and
bottles

SWEET CAKES SOAP, INC.
www.sweetcakes.com
(973) 838-5200
(973) 838-9925 fax
• supplier of essential and fragrance oils

SWEET PRAIRIE SOAP COMPANY
www.sweetprairiesoap.com
130 North 28th St.
Quincy, IL 62301
(217) 222-1099
(702) 995-5717 fax
(877) 651-9416 orders only
• supplier of handcrafted soap and bath
products

TKB TRADING, LLC
www.tkbtrading.com
356 24th St.
Oakland, CA 94612
(510) 451-9011
• supplier of soapmaking supplies, including colorants

**UNIVERSITY OF WASHINGTON'S
MEDICINAL HERB GARDEN**
www.nnlm.nlm.nih.gov/pnr/uwmhg/
• information on herbs

WENNER'S WOOD & METAL, INC.
www.woodandmetal.com
2001 Jefferson Hwy.
Fishersville, VA 22939
(540) 943-6633 phone/fax
• supplier of soap molds and cutters

WHOLESALESUPPLIESPLUS.COM INC.
www.wholesalesuppliesplus.com
13390 York Rd., Unit G
North Royalton, Ohio 44133
(800) 359-0944
(440) 237-0639 fax
• wholesale supplier of soapmaking supplies, including colorants, fragrances and
base soaps

YE OLDE SOAP SHOPPE
www.soapmaking.com
15602 Old Highway 80
Flinn Springs, California 92021
(800) 390-9969 orders only
(619) 390-3525
(619) 390-7148 fax
(619) 390-1523 farm phone
(619) 390-0912 farm fax
• supplier of soapmaking supplies, molds,
kits and handcrafted soap

ZENITH SUPPLIES
www.zenithsupplies.com
6300 Roosevelt Way NE
Seattle, WA
(800) 735-7217
(206) 525-3703 fax
• supplier of essential and fragrance oils,
base oils, herbs, lotions and creams

Index

Try your hand at these other fun crafts—
NORTH LIGHT BOOKS MAKES IT EASY!

Create Your Own Tabletop Fountains

You can create your own tabletop fountains and add beautiful accents to your living room, bedroom, kitchen and garden. These 15 gorgeous step-by-step projects make it easy, using everything from lava rock and bamboo to shells and clay pots. You'll learn to incorporate flowers, driftwood, fire, figurines, crystals, plants and more to create works of art that will have friends buzzing for years to come.

ISBN 1-58180-103-3, paperback, 128 pages, #31791-K

Fabric Crafts

Create unique, colorful crafts, including greeting cards, journal covers, picture frames, wall hangings and more with a world of exciting fabrics. All you need to get started are some old clothes, buttons, coins, cording, faux jewelry and other embellishments. Simple decorative techniques, such as fabric stamping, collage and basic stitching, are clearly explained inside, requiring no prior knowledge of sewing or quilting.

ISBN 1-58180-153-X, paperback, 128 pages, #31902-K

Easy Mosaics for Your Home and Garden

You can create a range of decorative mosaics for your home and garden! These twenty exciting projects include step-by-step instructions, materials lists and templates you can enlarge and trace. There's no tile to cut and no messy grout. Just pick a project and get creative! From garden stepping stones to table tops, you'll find beautiful mosaic projects for every part of your home.

ISBN 1-58180-129-7, paperback, 128 pages, #31830-K

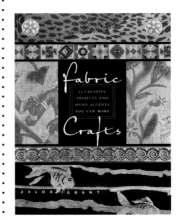

Enchanting Woodland Birdhouses

Create rustic, whimsical houses perfect for use indoors and out. Lucinda Macy provides step-by-step instructions and full-color photos that make every project easy. There are 13 designs in all, including birdhouses, decorative fairy and gnome homes, and garden homes for toads. Each one can be embellished with acorns, moss, seedpods, twigs and other natural materials.

ISBN 1-58180-071-1, paperback, 128 pages, #31793-K

These books and other fine North Light titles are available from your local art & craft retailer, bookstore, online supplier or by calling 1-800-448-0915.